ॐ

SANSKRIT NOUN DECLENSION
using Ashtadhyayi Sutras

Ashwini Kumar Aggarwal

edited by

SADHVI HEMSWAROOPA

जय गुरुदेव

ISBN13: 978-93-92201-91-2 Paperback Edition
ISBN13: 978-93-92201-92-9 Hardbound Edition
ISBN13: 978-93-92201-94-3 Digital Edition

Title: **Sanskrit Noun declension using Ashtadhyayi Sutras**
Author: **Ashwini Kumar Aggarwal**

Printed and Published by
Devotees of Sri Sri Ravi Shankar Ashram
34 Sunny Enclave, Devigarh Road,
Patiala 147001, Punjab, India

https://advaita56.weebly.com/
The Art of Living Centre

https://www.artofliving.org/

14th January 2022 Makara Sankranti, Pongal, Bihu, Lohri
Shukla Paksha Kurma Dvadashi, Uttarayana, Rohini Nakshatra,
Vikram Samvat 2078 Ananda, Saka Era 1943 Plava

1st Edition January 2022

जय गुरुदेव

Dedication

Sri Sri Ravi Shankar

who allows us to explore new words with good cheer

Blessing

In Sanskrit, 'Apaha' means both water & love. 'Aptah' is dear one. Water, life & love are inseparable. Let's keep them pure.

Sri Sri Ravi Shankar
7:18 am Mar 23, 2017 @SriSri Twitter for iPhone

Acknowledgements

Mataji Brahmaprakasananda of AVG Nagpur, for superb teaching.
Pushpa Maa of Panini Shodh Sansthan, for excelling in Sanskrit.

Prayer

शान्तिपाठः

ॐ सह नाववतु । सह नौ भुनक्तु । सह वीर्यं करवावहै ।

तेजस्वि नावधीतमस्तु मा विद्विषावहै ॥

ॐ शान्तिः शान्तिः शान्तिः ॥

oṃ saha nāvavatu | saha nau bhunaktu | saha vīryaṃ karavāvahai |

tejasvi nāvadhītamastu mā vidviṣāvahai ||

oṃ śānti śānti śāntiḥ ||

Peace Invocation

O Pure Loving Grace!

May we be taken care of along with our family and friends.
May we enjoy socializing and eating together.
May we support each other's vision and growth.
May our intellect be open to new ideas and changing trends.
May we spend more time in praise than abuse, may we talk of each other's virtues rather than harp on vices.

Peace in our heart, in our body and in our environs.

Table of Contents

BLESSING **3**

PRAYER **4**

PREFACE **12**

MASCULINE अ इ उ ऋ ऐ ओ औ STEM FINAL VOWEL **17**

राम Rama, Lord 18
हरि Hari, Vishnu, Lord, Success giver 19
पति Husband, Consort, Boss 20
सखि Friend, Companion, colleague, roommate 21
गुरु Guru, Acharya, Master, Remover of Ignorance 22
दातृ Donatee, Giver of Charity, Lord who fulfills 23
पितृ Father, Guardian, head of family 24
रै Resources, Wealth 25
गो Bull, Cow, Ox 26
ग्लौ Moon, Pleasant Shining Light, Nourisher 27

FEMININE आ इ ई उ ऊ ऋ ऐ ओ औ STEM FINAL VOWEL **28**

रमा Consort of Lord, Goddess of Wealth, Fair Maiden 29
मति Intellect, thought, reasoning, opinion 30
नदी River, flowing current 32
श्री endowed with Wealth, Resourceful 33
स्त्री woman, one needing an anchor, wife 34
धेनु Cow, milch animal 35
वधू bride, newly wed girl 36
भू earth, planet that sustains life 37
स्वसृ Sister, affectionate girl 38
मातृ Mother, giver of birth 39
रै Resources, Wealth 40
गो Bull, Cow, Ox 41
नौ Boat. ferry 42

NEUTER अ इ उ ऋ STEM FINAL VOWEL 43

फल fruit, natural delicacy 44
वारि water, clear liquid 45
दधि curd. yoghurt 46
शुचि pure, clean 47
गुरु heavy, bulky, stressful, weight bearing 48
मधु honey, natural sweetner 50
दातृ That which gives, pot gives water 51

MASCULINE च् ज् त् द् न् श् ष् स् ह् STEM FINAL CONSONANT 52

जलमुच् Cloud, airy ball of water 53
वणिज् Merchant, trader 54
राज् King, Head, President 55
Masculine stems त् ending 56
मरुत् Wind, Hanuman, Speedy 58
पचत् Cook, Chef 60
धीमत् Intelligent, talented, genius 62
महत् Great, magnificient, noble 63
सुहृद् Friend, affectionate one, good at heart 64
राजन् King 65
आत्मन् Soul, inner purity, Jiva 66
श्वन् Dog, Canine 69
युवन् Youth, Teenager मघवन् Storm cloud, Lord Indra 70
पथिन् Road, path, journey करिन् elephant 71
विश् People, crowd, group of humans 72
तादृश् Such, like that, likewise 73
द्विष् Enemy, one who harbors ill-will, bitter person 74
वेधस् all-knowledgeable, Lord Brahma, Creator 75
श्रेयस् Superior, Ultimate 76
विद्वस् Scholar, professor 77
पुम्स् = पुंस् Man, male of species 78

दोस् Arm, forearm (body part) 79
लिह् One who licks, baby like, puppy like 80

FEMININE च् ज् त् ध् न् प् भ् र् व् श् ष् स् ह् STEM FINAL CONSONANT 81

Declension Templates for Feminine नदी , रमा 82
वाच् Speech, Organ of speech 83
स्रज् garland 84
सरित् River, stream, Flowing current शरद् Autumn, Season 85
क्षुध् Hunger, Starvation 86
सीमन् Boundary, limit (has two declension forms) 87
अप् Waters, water sources 89
ककुभ् Region 90
पुर् town, city 91
दिव् Heaven 92
निश् Night दिश् Direction 93
प्रावृष् Rainy season, Monsoon 94
भास् Light, illumination, understanding आशिस् Blessing, grace 95
उपानह् Shoe, Belly 95

NEUTER च् ज् त् द् न् श् ष् स् ह् STEM FINAL CONSONANT 96

सुवाच् Eloquent speech, oratory 97
असृज् 98
जगत् world, society 99
ददत् act of giving charity तुदत् act of giving pain 100
पचत् act of cooking 101
महत् massive, huge, great 102
हृद् heart, core, blueprint of something 102
नामन् name, surname, formal name, label 103
कर्मन् action ब्रह्मन् supreme consciousness 104
अहन् day (duration between 6am to 6pm) 105
गुणिन् meritorious 106
वार् water, still waters, deep blue sea 107

तादृश् likewise....107
सुत्विष् shiny, glowing, lustrous....108
मनस् mind, thoughts, opinion हविस् Oblation....109
वपुस् body, trunk तस्थिवस् that which stands steadfast, pillar....110
अभ्भोरुह् lotus, flower that grows in water....111

SARVANAMA (35 PRONOUN STEMS IN GANAPATHA)....112

Pronoun Stems & Sutras....113
Pronoun Gender Stems....114
Sutras for Sarvanama-Sthana Affixes....117
सर्व mfn - All, Everyone, Several (mfn, adjective usage)....118
सर्वा feminine - All, Everyone....119
सर्व neuter - All, Everyone....120
विश्व mfn – (declines as सर्व)....121
उभ mfn - both, the two, pair (only in Dual)....121
उभय mfn - to both sides, in two ways (has no Dual)....122
उभयी feminine (has no Dual)....123
उभय neuter (has no Dual)....124
डतर mf – (कतर यतर ततर decline as सर्व)....125
कतर n – who or what out of two (interrogative usage)....125
डतम mf – (कतम यतम ततम decline as सर्व)....126
कतम n – who or what out of many (interrogative)....126
अन्य mf – (declines as सर्व)....127
अन्य n – (declines as सर्व 3rd case onwards)....127
अन्यतर mf – (declines as सर्व)....127
अन्यतर n – (declines as सर्व 3rd case onwards)....127
इतर mf – (declines as सर्व)....127
इतर n – (declines as सर्व 3rd case onwards)....127
त्वत् mf – Other, other one, other thing....128
त्वत् n – Other, other thing....129
त्व mfn – (declines as सर्व)....131
नेम mn - One half, a portion....131
नेमा f - One half, a portion....132

सम mfn – one other portion (declines as सर्व) 132
सिम mfn – another part (declines as सर्व) 132
पूर्व Prior, Eastern (mfn, adjective usage, पूर्वा f , पूर्व n) 133
पर अवर दक्षिण उत्तर अपर अध (decline as पूर्व) 134
स्व One's own, oneself, personal possesion 134
अन्तर (declines as पूर्व) 134
त्यद् (declines as तद्) 134
तद् एतद् m 135
तद् एतद् f 136
तद् एतद् n 137
यद् mn 138
यद् f - Who, the one that 138
इदम् mn 139
इदम् f 140
अदस् mn 140
अदम् f 141
एक a, the (declines as सर्व) 142
द्वि mfn – the two, pair, both (only in Dual) 143
युष्मद् mfn – YOU (personal pronoun) 144
अस्मद् mfn – I (personal pronoun) 145
भवत् m - Thee, your honour, respectful address 146
भवती f - Thee, your honour, respectful address 147
भवत् n – a revered thing, a photograph/statue 148
किम् mfn - who, what (interrogative usage) 149
किम् f - who, what (interrogative usage) 150
किम् neuter - who, what (interrogative usage) 151

NUMERAL CARDINALS सङ्ख्या 1, 2, 3 152

एक one 153
द्वि two 153
त्रि three 154
चतुर् four 154

पञ्चन् षन् सप्तन् – five six seven 155
अष्टन् eight 155
नवन् दशन् एकादशन् द्वादशन् – nine ten eleven twelve 156
त्रयोदशन् चतुर्दशन् पञ्चदशन् षोडशन् – thirteen fourteen fifteen sixteen 156
सप्तदशन् अष्टदशन् नवदशन् – seventeen eighteen nineteen 157
कति mfn – How many Number? How much Quantity? 157

NUMERAL ORDINALS सङ्ख्येय 1ST, 2ND, 3RD 158

प्रथम m - First, 1st, Initial 158
प्रथमा f - First, Initial 159
प्रथम n - First, Initial 160
द्वितीय m – Second, 2nd, Latter तृतीय Third 161
द्वितीया f – Second, 2nd, Latter तृतीया Third, 3rd 162
द्वितीय n – Second, 2nd, Latter तृतीय Third, 3rd 163
चतुर्थ m - Fourth, 4th, Transcendental State 164
तुरीय m - Fourth, 4th, Transcendental State 164
चतुर्थी f – Fourth, 4th, Transcendental State 165
तुरीया f – Fourth, 4th, Transcendental State 165
चतुर्थ n – Fourth, 4th, Transcendental State 166
तुरीय n – Fourth, 4th, Transcendental State 166
पञ्चम m - Fifth, 5th, onwards 6th, 7th… 100th etc 167
पञ्चमी f - Fifth, 5th, onwards 6th, 7th… 100th etc 167
पञ्चम n – Fifth, 5th, onwards 6th, 7th… 100th etc 168

IRREGULAR STEMS IN MASC WITH FINAL VOWEL विशेष शब्द पुंलिङ्गः 169

ऐक्ष्वाक m - First, 1st, Initial 169
निर्जर m - Lord, Unageing, Never becoming old 169
पाद m – Foot (body part), quarter 170
दन्त m – Tooth (body part) 170
मास m – month, 30 day period 171
विश्वपा m - Lord, Protector of World 172

GENDER OF WORDS MASCULINE/FEMININE/NEUTER.........................175

MASCULINE/FEMININE/NEUTER सुप् प्रत्यय TABLE.................................176

7x3 Masculine/Feminine सुप् प्रत्यय table without Tag 176
7x3 Neuter सुप् प्रत्यय table without Tag 177
7x3 सुप् प्रत्यय Mechanics of Tag letters.. 178
सुप् प्रत्यय Affixes modified in use by Sutras 179
Masc feminine सर्वनामस्थानं प्रत्यय Sarvanamasthana Affixes 180
Neuter नपुंसकस्य सर्वनामस्थानं प्रत्यय Sarvanamasthana Affixes 181
5+1 सर्वनामस्थानं प्रत्यय Sarvanamasthana Affixes 182
हलादि प्रत्यय Affixes having Initial Consonant.................................... 183
Anga facing these Sup affixes gets पदम् Technical Name................ 184
mf Anga facing these Sup affixes gets भ Technical Name.............. 184
Karaka Vibhakti table.. 186

RELEVANT ASHTADHYAYI SUTRAS 188
RELEVANT TECHNICAL TERMS 188
PLACE & EFFORT OF ENUNCIATION 190
MAHESHWAR SUTRAS W.R.T. PRATYAHARAS 192
LATIN TRANSLITERATION CHART...193
SANSKRIT GRAMMAR 194
CONJUGATION PROCESS OF VERB...197
DECLENSION PROCESS OF NOUN 198
REFERENCES...199
अष्टाध्यायी सहजबोध VOL 5...199
EPILOGUE..200

Preface

Sanskrit is coming of Age. More and more Colleges and Universities are offering a degree course in this lingua franca of yore.

Many schools across Europe and America are introducing Sanskrit to young learners.

In India too there is a revival across the length and breadth, with committed organisations working to reach out to adults and children all over.

To understand Sanskrit Grammar, the basic stuff is all about knowing the correct spelling of NOUNS and VERBS. This edition gives the correct spelling of all Sanskrit NOUNS, that are seen in literature. It also goes into the Ashtadhyayi of Panini to see what changes are involved to make the final spelling.

The 7x3 Sup Table matrices for Nouns in 7 cases and 3 numbers are judiciously arranged, with emphasis on clarity and legibility. Gender of Nouns is explicitly specified, and the mechanism of original Sup Affixes, and Modified Sup affixes is elaborated.

Ashtadhyayi Sutras for Sandhi changes in the Noun spellings are listed, so that the reader understands the background process threadbare.

The Ashtadhyayi of Panini and Ancillary Texts

- Dhatupatha text lists the Roots.
- Ganapatha text lists many Noun Stems.
- Linga Anushasana text gives criteria for gender of stems.
- The Ashtadhyayi of Panini lists the Affixes and Upasargas (prefixes) that attach to Roots for construction of Nouns and Verbs.

Masculine NOUN flowchart

- Dhatu + Krit affix → Pratipadika + Sup affix → Noun
- Dhatu + Unadi affix → Pratipadika + Sup affix → Noun

Note

- Pratipadika = Noun STEM

Feminine NOUN Flowchart

- Dhatu + Krit affix → Pratipadika + Feminine affix → Pratipadika^{f} + Sup affix → Noun
- Dhatu + Unadi affix → Pratipadika^{f} + Sup affix → Noun

Neuter NOUN Flowchart

Some stems are classified as both masculine and neuter, so the same masculine stem gets defined as a neuter stem, and uses Sutras from the Ashtadhyayi meant for neuter stems. There aren't specific affixes to make neuter stems.

- Dhatu + Krit affix → Pratipadika^{n} + Sup affix → Noun
- Dhatu + Unadi affix → Pratipadika^{n} + Sup affix → Noun

Vocative Case

It is not defined as a distinct case, rather some sutras in the Ashtadhyayi help in the construction of Vocative. It is only used in the Nominative sense. Usually the Vocative Singular is seen in literature, and it is called Sambuddhi. However we also decline the Vocative dual and plural, which is identical to the Nominative dual and plural respectively.

7x3 Sup Noun Affixes Matrix by Sutra 4.1.2

V हे	V/1	V/2	V/3	similar to Nominative		
1	1/1	1/2	1/3	स् उँ	औ	ज् अस्
2	2/1	2/2	2/3	अम्	औ ट्	श् अस्
3	3/1	3/2	3/3	ट् आ	भ्याम्	भिस्
4	4/1	4/2	4/3	ङ् ए	भ्याम्	भ्यस्
5	5/1	5/2	5/3	ङ् अस् इँ	भ्याम्	भ्यस्
6	6/1	6/2	6/3	ङ् अस्	ओस्	आम्
7	7/1	7/2	7/3	ङ् इ	ओस्	सु प्

7x3 Sup Noun Affixes Matrix without Tag Letters

V हे	V/1	V/2	V/3	similar to Nominative		
1	1/1	1/2	1/3	स्	औ	अस्
2	2/1	2/2	2/3	अम्	औ	अस्
3	3/1	3/2	3/3	आ	भ्याम्	भिस्
4	4/1	4/2	4/3	ए	भ्याम्	भ्यस्
5	5/1	5/2	5/3	अस्	भ्याम्	भ्यस्
6	6/1	6/2	6/3	अस्	ओस्	आम्
7	7/1	7/2	7/3	इ	ओस्	सु

7x3 Sup Nouns Names

V हे	V/1 Vocative Singular	V/2 Vocative dual	V/3 Vocative plural
case / number	**1 singular number**	**2 dual number**	**3 plural number**
1 Nominative case	1/1 Nominative Singular	1/2 Nominative dual	1/3 Nominative plural
2 Accusative case	2/1 Accusative Singular	2/2 Accusative dual	2/3 Accusative plural
3 Instrumental case	3/1 Instrumental Singular	3/2 Instrumental dual	3/3 Instrumental plural
4 Dative case	4/1 Dative Singular	4/2 Dative dual	4/3 Dative plural
5 Ablative case	5/1 Ablative Singular	5/2 Ablative dual	5/3 Ablative plural
6 Genitive case	6/1 Genitive Singular	6/2 Genitive dual	6/3 Genitive plural
7 Locative case	7/1 Locative Singular	7/2 Locative dual	7/3 Locative plural

7x3 सुप् नामन् Sanskrit Names

V **हे**	V/1 सम्बुद्धिः	V/2 सम्बोधनम् द्विवचनम्	V/3 सम्बोधनम् बहुवचनम्
विभक्ति / वचन	**1** **एकवचनम्**	**2** **द्विवचनम्**	**3** **बहुवचनम्**
1st **प्रथमा विभक्तिः**	1/1 प्रथमम् एकवचनम्	1/2 प्रथमम् द्विवचनम्	1/3 प्रथमम् बहुवचनम्
2nd **द्वितीया विभक्तिः**	2/1 द्वितीया एकवचनम्	2/2 द्वितीया द्विवचनम्	2/3 द्वितीया बहुवचनम्
3rd **तृतीया विभक्तिः**	3/1 तृतीया एकवचनम्	3/2 तृतीया द्विवचनम्	3/3 तृतीया बहुवचनम्
4th **चतुर्थी विभक्तिः**	4/1 चतुर्थी एकवचनम्	4/2 चतुर्थी द्विवचनम्	4/3 चतुर्थी बहुवचनम्
5th **पञ्चमी विभक्तिः**	5/1 पञ्चमी एकवचनम्	5/2 पञ्चमी द्विवचनम्	5/3 पञ्चमी बहुवचनम्
6th **षष्ठी विभक्तिः**	6/1 षष्ठी एकवचनम्	6/2 षष्ठी द्विवचनम्	6/3 षष्ठी बहुवचनम्
7th **सप्तमी विभक्तिः**	7/1 सप्तमी एकवचनम्	7/2 सप्तमी द्विवचनम्	7/3 सप्तमी बहुवचनम्

Masculine अ इ उ ऋ ऐ ओ औ stem final Vowel

अजन्तः पुंलिङ्गः शब्दाः wrt Maheshwar Sutras

अ, इ , उ	अ इ उ ण्	1
ऋ	ऋ ऌ क्	2
ऐ	ए ओ ङ्	3
ओ, औ	ऐ औ च्	4
	हयवरट्	5
	लँण्	6
	ञमङणनम्	7
	झभञ्	8
	घढधष्	9
	जबगडदश्	10
	खफछठथचटतव्	11
	कपय्	12
	शषसर्	13
	हल्	14

Note

- Vocative dual and plural V/2, V/3 are usually identically declined as Nominative 1/2, 1/3.
- Vocative singular V/1 is termed सम्बुद्धिः and special sutras may apply.

राम Rama, Lord

राम	र् आ म् अ = masculine stem अ ending, अकारान्तः			सुप् Affixes		
V हे	राम 6.1.69	रामौ	रामाः	similar to Nominative		
	1	2	3	1	2	3
1	रामः 8.2.66 8.3.15	रामौ 6.1.88	रामाः 6.1.102 8.2.66 8.3.15	स्	औ	अस्
2	रामम् 6.1.107	रामौ 6.1.88	रामान् 6.1.102 6.1.103	अम्	औ	अस्
3	रामेण 7.1.12 6.1.87 8.4.2	रामाभ्याम् 7.3.102	रामैः 7.1.9 6.1.88 8.2.66 8.3.15	आ	भ्याम्	भिस्
4	रामाय 7.1.13 7.3.102	रामाभ्याम् 7.3.102	रामेभ्यः 7.3.103 8.2.66 8.3.15	(ङ्) ए	भ्याम्	भ्यस्
5	रामात् 7.1.12 6.1.101	रामाभ्याम् 7.3.102	रामेभ्यः 7.3.103 8.2.66 8.3.15	ङ् अस् ङँ	भ्याम्	भ्यस्
6	रामस्य 7.1.12	रामयोः 7.3.104 6.1.78 8.2.66 8.3.15	रामाणाम् 7.1.54 6.4.3 8.4.2	(ङ्) अस्	ओस्	आम्
7	रामे 6.1.87	रामयोः 7.3.104 6.1.78 8.2.66 8.3.15	रामेषु 7.3.103 8.3.59	(ङ्) इ	ओस्	सु
Similar stems देव God, मुकुन्द Krishna, शिव, हर Shiva, बालक Boy						

हरि Hari, Vishnu, Lord, Success giver

हरि	ह् अ र् इ = masculine stem इ ending, इकारान्तः		
V हे	हरे 7.3.108 6.1.69	हरी	हरयः
1	हरिः 8.2.66 8.3.15	हरी 6.1.102	हरयः 7.3.109 6.1.105 6.1.78 8.2.66 8.3.15
2	हरिम् 6.1.107	हरी 6.1.102	हरीन् 6.1.102 6.1.103
3	हरिणा 7.3.120 8.4.2	हरिभ्याम्	हरिभिः 8.2.66 8.3.15
4	हरये 7.3.111 6.1.78	हरिभ्याम्	हरिभ्यः 8.2.66 8.3.15
5	हरेः 7.3.111 6.1.110 8.2.66 8.3.15	हरिभ्याम्	हरिभ्यः 8.2.66 8.3.15
6	हरेः 7.3.111 6.1.110 8.2.66 8.3.15	हर्योः 6.1.77 8.2.66 8.3.15	हरीणाम् 7.1.54 6.4.3 8.4.2
7	हरौ 7.3.119 6.1.88	हर्योः 6.1.77 8.2.66 8.3.15	हरिषु 8.3.59
Similar stems रवि sun, कवि poet, मुनि sage, विधि fate, श्रीपति Vishnu, अग्नि fire			
In 3/1, 4/1, 6/2, 7/2 we see appearance of यकार। It is the samprasarana equivalent of इकार।			

पति Husband, Consort, Boss

पति	प् अ त् इ = इकारान्तः		m
V हे	पते 7.3.108 6.1.69	पती	पतयः
1	पतिः 8.2.66 8.3.15	पती 6.1.102	पतयः 7.3.109 6.1.105 6.1.78 8.2.66 8.3.15
2	पतिम् 6.1.107	पती 6.1.102	पतीन् 6.1.102 6.1.103
3	पत्या 1.4.8 6.1.77	पतिभ्याम्	पतिभिः 8.2.66 8.3.15
4	पत्ये 1.4.8 6.1.77	पतिभ्याम्	पतिभ्यः 8.2.66 8.3.15
5	पत्युः 1.4.8 6.1.77 6.1.112 8.2.66 8.3.15	पतिभ्याम्	पतिभ्यः 8.2.66 8.3.15
6	पत्युः 1.4.8 6.1.77 6.1.112 8.2.66 8.3.15	पत्योः 6.1.77 8.2.66 8.3.15	पतिनाम् 7.1.54 6.4.3
7	पत्यो 1.4.8 6.1.77	पत्योः 6.1.77 8.2.66 8.3.15	पतिषु 8.3.59
3/1 4/1 5/1 6/1 7/1 are different from हरि as seen in literature. The sutra 7.3.120 is not applied due to 1.4.8. So यण् sandhi 6.1.77 gets applied			

पति and सखि are irregular words in इकारान्त । However the word पति is declined exactly like हरि when it stands at the end of a compound. E.g. stems सीतापति, भूपति, नृपति, श्रीपति are identical to हरि ।

सखि Friend, Companion, colleague, roommate

सखि	= स् अ ख् इ = इकारान्तः		m
V हे	सखे 7.3.108 6.1.69	सखायौ	सखायः
1	सखा 7.1.92 7.1.93 6.4.8 6.1.68 8.2.7	सखायौ 7.1.92 7.2.115	सखायः 7.1.92 7.2.115 6.1.78 8.2.66 8.3.15
2	सखायम् 7.1.92 7.2.115 6.1.78	सखायौ 7.1.92 7.2.115	सखीन्
3	सख्या 1.4.7 6.1.77	सखिभ्याम्	सखिभिः 8.2.66 8.3.15
4	सख्ये 1.4.7 6.1.77	सखिभ्याम्	सखिभ्यः 8.2.66 8.3.15
5	सख्युः 1.4.7 6.1.77 6.1.112 8.2.66 8.3.15	सखिभ्याम्	सखिभ्यः 8.2.66 8.3.15
6	सख्युः 1.4.7 6.1.77 6.1.112 8.2.66 8.3.15	सख्योः 6.1.77 8.2.66 8.3.15	सखीनाम् 7.1.54 6.4.3
7	सख्यौ 7.3.119 6.1.88	सख्योः 6.1.77 8.2.66 8.3.15	सखिषु 8.3.59
1/1 2/1 3/1, 1/2 2/2 2/3, are different from हरि due to 7.1.92, 1/3 1/4 1/5 1/6 1/7 are different from हरि since 7.3.120 is not applied due to 1.4.7. Thus यण् sandhi gets applied.			

गुरु Guru, Acharya, Master, Remover of Ignorance

गुरु	ग् उ र् उ = उकारान्तः		m
V हे	गुरो 7.3.108 6.1.69	गुरू	गुरवः
1	गुरुः 8.2.66 8.3.15	गुरू 6.1.102	गुरवः 7.3.109 6.1.105 6.1.78 8.2.66 8.3.15
2	गुरुम् 6.1.107	गुरू 6.1.102	गुरून् 6.1.102 6.1.103
3	गुरुणा 7.3.120 8.4.2	गुरुभ्याम्	गुरुभिः 8.2.66 8.3.15
4	गुरवे 7.3.111 6.1.78	गुरुभ्याम्	गुरुभ्यः 8.2.66 8.3.15
5	गुरोः 7.3.111 6.1.110 8.2.66 8.3.15	गुरुभ्याम्	गुरुभ्यः 8.2.66 8.3.15
6	गुरोः 7.3.111 6.1.110 8.2.66 8.3.15	गुर्वोः 6.1.77 8.2.66 8.3.15	गुरूणाम् 7.1.54 6.4.3 8.4.2
7	गुरौ 7.3.119 6.1.88	गुर्वोः 6.1.77 8.2.66 8.3.15	गुरुषु 8.3.59
Teacher, preceptor, visionary, advisor			
शम्भु Shiva, विष्णु Vishnu, भानु sun, सूनु son			
In 3/1, 4/1, 6/2, 7/2 we see appearance of वकार । It is the samprasarana equivalent of उकार ।			

दातृ Donatee, Giver of Charity, Lord who fulfills

दातृ	द् आ त् ऋ = ऋकारान्तः		m
V हे	दातः 2.3.49 7.3.110 1.1.51 6.1.68 8.3.15	दातारौ	दातारः
1	दाता 7.1.94 6.4.8 6.1.68 8.2.7	दातारौ 7.3.110 1.1.51 6.4.11	दातारः 7.3.110 1.1.51 6.4.11 8.2.66 8.3.15
2	दातारम् 7.3.110 1.1.51 6.4.11	दातारौ 7.3.110 1.1.51 6.4.11	दातॄन् 6.1.102 6.1.103
3	दात्रा 6.1.77	दातृभ्याम्	दातृभिः 8.2.66 8.3.15
4	दात्रे 6.1.77	दातृभ्याम्	दातृभ्यः 8.2.66 8.3.15
5	दातुः 6.1.111 8.2.24 8.3.15	दातृभ्याम्	दातृभ्यः 8.2.66 8.3.15
6	दातुः 6.1.111 8.2.24 8.3.15	दात्रोः 6.1.77 8.2.66 8.3.15	दातॄणाम् 7.1.54 6.4.8 3.4.2 Vartika
7	दातरि 7.3.110 1.1.51	दात्रोः 6.1.77 8.2.66 8.3.15	दातृषु 8.3.59
नेतृ leader, कर्तृ doer, धातृ Creator, वक्तृ speaker, नप्तृ grandson. In 1/2 1/3 2/1 2/2 3/1 4/1 6/2 7/1 7/2 we see appearance of रेफ, samprasarana equivalent of ऋकार ।			

This is the template for Agent nouns, formed from dhatus. Almost all the 1943 dhatus can be used in this way, in the sense of Doership.

These nouns form their feminine by addition of ई e.g. दात्री, नेत्री, धात्री, कर्त्री and decline like नदी ।

पितृ Father, Guardian, head of family

पितृ	प् इ त् ऋ = ऋकारान्तः		m
V हे	पितः 2.3.49 7.3.110 1.1.51 6.1.68 8.3.15	पितरौ 7.3.110 1.1.51	पितरः 7.3.110 1.1.51 8.2.66 8.3.15
1	पिता 7.1.94 6.4.8 6.1.68 8.2.7	पितरौ 7.3.110 1.1.51	पितरः 7.3.110 1.1.51 8.2.66 8.3.15
2	पितरम् 7.3.110 1.1.51	पितरौ 7.3.110 1.1.51	पितॄन् 6.1.102 6.1.103
3	पित्रा 6.1.77	पितृभ्याम्	पितृभिः
4	पित्रे 6.1.77	पितृभ्याम्	पितृभ्यः
5	पितुः 6.1.111 1.1.51 8.2.24 8.3.15	पितृभ्याम्	पितृभ्यः
6	पितुः 6.1.111 1.1.51 8.2.24 8.3.15	पित्रोः 6.1.77 8.2.66 8.3.15	पितॄणाम् 7.1.54 6.4.3
7	पितरि 7.3.110 1.1.51	पित्रोः 6.1.77 8.2.66 8.3.15	पितृषु 8.3.59
Identical to दातृ except for 1/2 1/3 2/2			
भ्रातृ brother,जामातृ son-in-law,देवृ husband's brother. Also other family relationships, सव्येष्टृ charioteer			
नृ man, declines identical to पितृ except its 6/3 case has the optional forms नृणाम् and नॄणाम् by 6.4.6			
नप्तृ grandson, declines like दातृ due to 6.4.11			

This is the template for family relationship nouns.

रै Resources, Wealth

रै	र् ऐ = ऐकारान्तः		m, f
V हे	राः	रायौ	रायः
1	राः 7.2.85 8.2.66 8.3.15	रायौ 6.1.105 6.1.78	रायः 6.1.105 6.1.78 8.2.66 8.3.15
2	रायम् 6.1.78	रायौ 6.1.105 6.1.78	रायः 6.1.105 6.1.78 8.2.66 8.3.15
3	राया 6.1.78	राभ्याम् 7.2.85	राभिः 7.2.85 8.2.66 8.3.15
4	राये 6.1.78	राभ्याम् 7.2.85	राभ्यः 7.2.85 8.2.66 8.3.15
5	रायः 6.1.78 8.2.66 8.3.15	राभ्याम् 7.2.85	राभ्यः 7.2.85 8.2.66 8.3.15
6	रायः 6.1.78 8.2.66 8.3.15	रायोः 6.1.78 8.2.66 8.3.15	रायाम् 6.1.78
7	रायि 6.1.78	रायोः 6.1.78 8.2.66 8.3.15	रासु 7.2.85

This word रै is used both in masculine sense and feminine sense. The declension is as above.

गो Bull, Cow, Ox

गो	ग् ओ = ओकारान्तः		m, f
V हे	गौः	गावौ	गावः
1	गौः 7.1.90 7.2.115 8.2.66 8.3.15	गावौ 7.1.90 7.2.115 6.1.105 6.1.78	गावः 7.1.90 7.2.115 6.1.105 6.1.78 8.2.66 8.3.15
2	गाम् 6.1.93	गावौ 7.1.90 7.2.115 6.1.105 6.1.78	गाः 6.1.93 8.2.66 8.3.15
3	गवा 6.1.78	गोभ्याम्	गोभिः 8.2.66 8.3.15
4	गवे 6.1.78	गोभ्याम्	गोभ्यः 8.2.66 8.3.15
5	गोः 6.1.110 8.2.66 8.3.15	गोभ्याम्	गोभ्यः 8.2.66 8.3.15
6	गोः 6.1.110 8.2.66 8.3.15	गवोः 6.1.78 8.2.66 8.3.15	गवाम् 6.1.78
7	गवि 6.1.78	गवोः 6.1.78 8.2.66 8.3.15	गोषु 8.3.59

This word गो is used both in masculine and feminine. The declension is as above.

ग्लौ Moon, Pleasant Shining Light, Nourisher

ग्लौ	ग् ल् औ = औकारान्तः		m
V हे	ग्लौः	ग्लावौ	ग्लावः
1	ग्लौः 8.2.66 8.3.15	ग्लावौ 6.1.105 6.1.78	ग्लावः 6.1.105 6.1.78 8.2.66 8.3.15
2	ग्लावम् 6.1.78	ग्लावौ 6.1.105 6.1.78	ग्लावः 6.1.78 8.2.66 8.3.15
3	ग्लावा 6.1.78	ग्लौभ्याम्	ग्लौभिः 8.2.66 8.3.15
4	ग्लावे 6.1.78	ग्लौभ्याम्	ग्लौभ्यः 8.2.66 8.3.15
5	ग्लावः 6.1.78 8.2.66 8.3.15	ग्लौभ्याम्	ग्लौभ्यः 8.2.66 8.3.15
6	ग्लावः 6.1.78 8.2.66 8.3.15	ग्लावोः 6.1.78 8.2.66 8.3.15	ग्लावाम् 6.1.78
7	ग्लावि 6.1.78	ग्लावोः 6.1.78 8.2.66 8.3.15	ग्लौषु 8.3.59

Feminine आ इ ई उ ऊ ऋ ऐ ओ औ stem final Vowel

अजन्तः स्त्रीलिङ्गः शब्दाः wrt Maheshwar Sutras

आ, इ, ई	अ इ उ ण्	1
उ, ऊ, ऋ	ऋ ऌ क्	2
ऐ	ए ओ ङ्	3
ओ, औ	ऐ औ च्	4
	हयवरट्	5
	लँण्	6
	ञमङणनम्	7
	झभञ्	8
	घढधष्	9
	जबगडदश्	10
	खफछठथचटतव्	11
	कपय्	12
	शषसर्	13
	हल्	14

Note

- अकारान्त words are Masculine or Neuter. Feminine words will be आकारान्त or ईकारान्त generally
- Feminine stems in ऐ ओ औ decline identically as their masculine counterparts
- Feminine आ affixes टाप् डाप् चाप् by 4.1.4, 4.1.13, 4.1.74
- Feminine ई affixes ङीप् ङीष् ङीन् by 4.1.5, 4.1.25, 4.1.73

रमा Consort of Lord, Goddess of Wealth, Fair Maiden

रमा	र् अ म् आ = आकारान्तः		f
V हे	रमे 7.3.106 6.1.68	रमे	रमाः
1	रमा 6.1.68	रमे 7.1.18 6.1.105 6.1.87	रमाः 6.1.105 6.1.101 8.2.66 8.3.15
2	रमाम् 6.1.107	रमे 7.1.18 6.1.105 6.1.87	रमाः 6.1.102 8.2.66 8.3.15
3	रमया 7.3.105 6.1.78	रमाभ्याम्	रमाभिः 8.2.66 8.3.15
4	रमायै 7.3.113 6.1.88	रमाभ्याम्	रमाभ्यः 8.2.66 8.3.15
5	रमायाः 7.3.113 6.1.101 8.2.66 8.3.15	रमाभ्याम्	रमाभ्यः 8.2.66 8.3.15
6	रमायाः 7.3.113 6.1.101 8.2.66 8.3.15	रमयोः 7.3.105 6.1.78 8.2.66 8.3.15	रमाणाम् 7.1.54 6.4.3 8.4.2
7	रमायाम् 7.3.116 7.3.113 6.1.101	रमयोः 7.3.105 6.1.78 8.2.66 8.3.15	रमासु
लता creeper, माला garland, सीता Sita, क्षमा forgiveness, लज्जा shame. Stems अम्बा अक्का अल्ला = mother, decline identical to रमा except for Vocative 1/1 which is हे अम्ब, हे अक्क, हे अल्ल resp. by 7.3.107			

For words that are used in the feminine sense, after the pratipadika has been constructed by a कृत् affix, it is made feminine by adding the आ affix.

4.1.4 अजाद्यतष्टाप् । टाप् = ट् आ प् । Without Tag letters it is आ affix.

मति Intellect, thought, reasoning, opinion

मति	म् अ त् इ = इकारान्तः		f
V हे	मते 7.3.108 6.1.69	मती	मतयः
1	मतिः 8.2.66 8.3.15	मती 6.1.102	मतयः 7.3.109 6.1.105 6.1.68 8.2.66 8.3.15
2	मतिम्	मती 6.1.102	मतीः 6.1.102 8.2.66 8.3.15
3	मत्या 6.1.77	मतिभ्याम्	मतिभिः 8.2.66 8.3.15
4	मत्यै / मतये 7.3.112 6.1.90 6.1.77 / 1.4.7 7.3.111 6.1.78	मतिभ्याम्	मतिभ्यः 8.2.66 8.3.15
5	मत्याः / मतेः 7.3.112 6.1.90 6.1.77 / 1.4.7 7.3.111 6.1.110	मतिभ्याम्	मतिभ्यः 8.2.66 8.3.15
6	मत्याः / मतेः 7.3.112 6.1.90 6.1.77 8.2.66 8.3.15 / 1.4.7 7.3.111 6.1.110 8.2.66 8.3.15	मत्योः 6.1.77 8.2.66 8.3.15	मतीनाम् 7.1.54 6.4.3
7	मत्याम् / मतौ 7.3.112 6.1.90 6.1.77 8.2.66 8.3.15 / 1.4.7 7.3.111 6.1.110 8.2.66 8.3.15	मत्योः 6.1.77 8.2.66 8.3.15	मतिषु 8.3.59
श्रुति Lord's voice,Vedas, रुचि taste, बुद्धि intellect, रात्रि night			
Template for abstract nouns in ति e.g. गति evolution, next life, कृति product, accomplishment, सृष्टि universe, creation			
4/1, 5/1, 6/1, 7/1 have two forms. This is generally true for feminine words ending in इ or उ ।			

4/1 Declension Process

मति ए 7.3.112 मति आ ए 6.1.90 मति ऐ 6.1.77 = मत्य् ऐ = मत्यै । or

मति ए 7.3.111 मते ए 6.1.78 मतय् ए = मतये ।

5/1, 6/1 Declension Process

मति अस् 7.3.112 मति आ अस् 6.1.90 मति आस् 6.1.77 = मत्य् आस् = मत्याः ।

मति अस् 7.3.111 मते अस् 6.1.110 मते स् 8.2.66 8.3.15 मतेः ।

7/1 Declension Process

मति इ 7.3.117 मति आम् 7.3.112 मति आ आम् 6.1.90 मति आम् 6.1.77 = मत्य् आम् = मत्याम् । or

मति इ 7.3.119 मत औ 6.1.88 मतौ ।

लक्ष्मी	ई	f
हे लक्ष्मि	हे लक्ष्म्यौ	हे लक्ष्म्यः
लक्ष्मीः	लक्ष्म्यौ	लक्ष्म्यः
लक्ष्मीम्	लक्ष्म्यौ	लक्ष्मीः
लक्ष्म्या	लक्ष्मीभ्यां	लक्ष्मीभिः
लक्ष्म्यै	लक्ष्मीभ्यां	लक्ष्मीभ्यः
लक्ष्म्याः	लक्ष्मीभ्यां	लक्ष्मीभ्यः
लक्ष्म्याः	लक्ष्म्योः	लक्ष्मीनां
लक्ष्म्यां	लक्ष्म्योः	लक्ष्मीषु
The stem लक्ष्मी is not affixed with ङीप् / ङीष् / ङीन् , hence 6.1.68 doesn't apply. Thus Nominative 1/1 form is different from नदी		

नदी River, flowing current

नदी	न् अ द् ई = ईकारान्तः		f
V हे	नदि 7.3.103 6.1.69	नद्यौ	नद्यः
1	नदी 6.1.68	नद्यौ 6.1.105 6.1.77	नद्यः 6.1.105 6.1.77 8.2.66 8.3.15
2	नदीम् 6.1.107	नद्यौ 6.1.105 6.1.77	नदीः 6.1.102 8.2.66 8.3.15
3	नद्या 6.1.77	नदीभ्याम्	नदीभिः 8.2.66 8.3.15
4	नद्यै 7.3.112 6.1.90 6.1.77	नदीभ्याम्	नदीभ्यः 8.2.66 8.3.15
5	नद्याः 7.3.112 6.1.90 6.1.77 8.2.66 8.3.15	नदीभ्याम्	नदीभ्यः 8.2.66 8.3.15
6	नद्याः 7.3.112 6.1.90 6.1.77 8.2.66 8.3.15	नद्योः 6.1.77 8.2.66 8.3.15	नदीनाम् 7.1.54 6.4.3
7	नद्याम् 7.3.116 6.1.77	नद्योः 6.1.77 8.2.66 8.3.15	नदीषु 8.3.59

गौरी lovely maiden, पार्वती Parvati/goddess of strength, सरस्वती goddess of wisdom, वाणी speech, सखी girl friend, देवी goddess

Template for feminine agent nouns in ई, eg कर्त्री doer, दात्री giver

4/1 = नदी ए 7.3.112 नदी आ ए 6.1.90 नदी ऐ 6.1.77 नद्य् ऐ = नद्यै ।

लक्ष्मी Lakshmi, goddess of fortune, अवी sun/air, तरी boat, तन्त्री lute, these stems decline identical to नदी except for 1/1 which is लक्ष्मीः अवीः तरीः तन्त्रीः since 6.1.68 doesn't apply as these stems are not ending in ङीप् / ङीष् / ङीन् affixes.

Also refer Karika that gives the seven stems not affixed with ङीप् / ङीष् / ङीन् , and so 6.1.68 doesn't apply.

अवी-तन्त्री-तरी-लक्ष्मी-ह्री-श्री-धी-नाम् उणादिषु । सप्तानाम् अपि शब्दानां सुँलोपो न कदाचन ॥ These stems are made from Unadi affixes.

श्री endowed with Wealth, Resourceful

श्री	श् र् ई = ईकारान्तः		f
V हे	श्रीः 1.4.4 8.2.66 8.3.15	श्रियौ	श्रियः
1	श्रीः 1.4.4 8.2.66 8.3.15	श्रियौ 1.4.4 6.4.77	श्रियः 6.4.77 8.2.66 8.3.15
2	श्रियम् 1.4.4 6.4.77	श्रियौ 1.4.4 6.4.77	श्रियः 6.4.77 8.2.66 8.3.15
3	श्रिया 1.4.4 6.4.77	श्रीभ्याम्	श्रीभिः 8.2.66 8.3.15
4	श्रियै / श्रिये 1.4.6 7.3.112 6.1.90 6.4.77 / 6.4.77	श्रीभ्याम्	श्रीभ्यः 8.2.66 8.3.15
5	श्रीयाः / श्रियः 1.4.6 6.1.90 6.4.77 8.2.66 8.3.15 / 6.4.77 8.2.66 8.3.15	श्रीभ्याम्	श्रीभ्यः 8.2.66 8.3.15
6	श्रीयाः / श्रियः 1.4.6 6.1.90 6.4.77 8.2.66 8.3.15 / 6.4.77 8.2.66 8.3.15	श्रियोः 6.4.77 8.2.66 8.3.15	श्रीणाम् / श्रियाम् 1.4.5 7.1.54 6.4.3 / 6.4.77
7	श्रियाम् / श्रियि 1.4.6 7.3.116 7.3.112 6.1.90 6.4.77 / 6.4.77	श्रियोः 6.4.77 8.2.66 8.3.15	श्रीषु 8.3.59
ह्री shame,धी intellect, भी fear			
6.1.68 doesn't apply as these stems are not ending in ङीप् / ङीष् / ङीन् affixes. 4/1 श्री ए 7.3.112 श्री आ ए 6.1.90 श्री ऐ 6.4.77 श्रिय् ऐ = श्रियै			

स्त्री woman, one needing an anchor, wife

स्त्री	स् त् र् ई = ईकारान्तः		f
V हे	स्त्रि 1.4.4 8.2.66 8.3.15	स्त्रियौ	स्त्रियः
1	स्त्री 6.1.68	स्त्रियौ 6.4.79	स्त्रियः 6.4.77 8.2.66 8.3.15
2	स्त्रियम् / स्त्रीम् 6.4.80 / 6.1.107	स्त्रियौ 6.4.79	स्त्रियः / स्त्रीः 6.4.80 8.2.66 8.3.15 / 6.1.102 8.2.66 8.3.15
3	स्त्रिया 6.4.79	स्त्रीभ्याम्	स्त्रीभिः 8.2.66 8.3.15
4	स्त्रियै 1.4.4 7.3.112 6.1.90 6.4.79	स्त्रीभ्याम्	स्त्रीभ्यः 8.2.66 8.3.15
5	स्त्रियाः 1.4.4 7.3.112 6.1.90 6.4.79 8.2.66 8.3.15	स्त्रीभ्याम्	स्त्रीभ्यः 8.2.66 8.3.15
6	स्त्रियाः 1.4.4 7.3.112 6.1.90 6.4.79 8.2.66 8.3.15	स्त्रियोः 6.4.79 8.2.66 8.3.15	स्त्रीणाम् 7.1.54 6.4.3 8.4.2
7	स्त्रियाम् 1.4.4 7.3.116 7.3.112 6.1.90 6.4.79	स्त्रियोः 6.4.79 8.2.66 8.3.15	स्त्रीषु 8.3.59

4/1 = स्त्री ए 7.3.112 स्त्री आ ए 6.1.90 स्त्री ऐ 6.4.79 स्त्रिय् ऐ = स्त्रियै ।

5/1, 6/1 = स्त्री अस् 7.3.112 स्त्री आ अस् 6.1.90 स्त्री आस् 6.4.79 स्त्रिय् आस् 8.2.66 स्त्रियार् 8.3.15 स्त्रियाः ।

7/1 = स्त्री इ 7.3.116 स्त्री आम् 7.3.112 स्त्री आ आम् 6.1.90 स्त्री आम् 6.4.79 स्त्रिय् आम् = स्त्रियाम् ।

धेनु Cow, milch animal

धेनु	ध् ए न् उ = उकारान्तः		f
V हे	धेनो 7.3.108 6.1.69	धेनू	धेनवः
1	धेनुः 8.2.66 8.3.15	धेनू 6.1.102	धेनवः 7.3.109 6.1.105 6.1.68 8.2.66 8.3.15
2	धेनुम्	धेनू 6.1.102	धेनूः 6.1.102 8.2.66 8.3.15
3	धेन्वा 6.1.77	धेनुभ्याम्	धेनुभिः 8.2.66 8.3.15
4	धेन्वै / धेनवे 7.3.112 6.1.90 6.1.77 / 1.4.7 7.3.111 6.1.78	धेनुभ्याम्	धेनुभ्यः 8.2.66 8.3.15
5	धेन्वाः / धेनोः 7.3.112 6.1.90 6.1.77 / 1.4.7 7.3.111 6.1.110	धेनुभ्याम्	धेनुभ्यः 8.2.66 8.3.15
6	धेन्वाः / धेनोः 7.3.112 6.1.90 6.1.77 8.2.66 8.3.15 / 1.4.7 7.3.111 6.1.110 8.2.66 8.3.15	धेन्वोः 6.1.77 8.2.66 8.3.15	धेनूनाम् 7.1.54 6.4.3
7	धेन्वाम् / धेनौ 7.3.112 6.1.90 6.1.77 8.2.66 8.3.15 / 1.4.7 7.3.111 6.1.110 8.2.66 8.3.15	धेन्वोः 6.1.77 8.2.66 8.3.15	धेनुषु 8.3.59
तनु body, इषु arrow, रज्जु rope, चञ्चु beak			
4/1, 5/1, 6/1, 7/1 have two forms. This is generally true for feminine words ending in इ or उ।			

As we can see, धेनु and मति decline similarly in all cases.

वधू bride, newly wed girl

वधू	व् अ ध् ऊ = ऊकारान्तः		f
V हे	वधु 7.3.103 6.1.69	वध्वौ	वध्वः
1	वधूः 8.2.66 8.3.15	वध्वौ 6.1.105 6.1.77	वध्वः 6.1.105 6.1.77 8.2.66 8.3.15
2	वधूम् 6.1.107	वध्वौ 6.1.105 6.1.77	वधूः 6.1.102 8.2.66 8.3.15
3	वध्वा 6.1.77	वधूभ्याम्	वधूभिः 8.2.66 8.3.15
4	वध्वै 7.3.112 6.1.90 6.1.77	वधूभ्याम्	वधूभ्यः 8.2.66 8.3.15
5	वध्वाः 7.3.112 6.1.90 6.1.77 8.2.66 8.3.15	वधूभ्याम्	वधूभ्यः 8.2.66 8.3.15
6	वध्वाः 7.3.112 6.1.90 6.1.77 8.2.66 8.3.15	वध्वोः 6.1.77 8.2.66 8.3.15	वधूनाम् 7.1.54 6.4.3
7	वध्वाम् 7.3.116 6.1.77	वध्वोः 6.1.77 8.2.66 8.3.15	वधूषु 8.3.59
चमू army, श्वश्रू mother-in-law			
Declines similar to नदी except for Nominative 1/1. Here 6.1.68 doesn't apply as वधू doesn't end in ङीप् / ङीष् / ङीन् affixes.			

भू earth, planet that sustains life

भू	भ् ऊ = ऊकारान्तः		f
V हे	भूः 1.4.4 8.2.66 8.3.15	भुवौ	भुवः
1	भूः 1.4.4 8.2.66 8.3.15	भुवौ 1.4.4 6.4.77	भुवः 6.4.77 8.2.66 8.3.15
2	भुवम् 1.4.4 6.4.77	भुवौ 1.4.4 6.4.77	भुवः 6.4.77 8.2.66 8.3.15
3	भुवा 1.4.4 6.4.77	भूभ्याम्	भूभिः 8.2.66 8.3.15
4	भुवै / भुवे 1.4.6 7.3.112 6.1.90 6.4.77 / 6.4.77	भूभ्याम्	भूभ्यः 8.2.66 8.3.15
5	भुवाः / भुवः 1.4.6 6.1.90 6.4.77 8.2.66 8.3.15 / 6.4.77 8.2.66 8.3.15	भूभ्याम्	भूभ्यः 8.2.66 8.3.15
6	भुवाः / भुवः 1.4.6 6.1.90 6.4.77 8.2.66 8.3.15 / 6.4.77 8.2.66 8.3.15	भुवोः 6.4.77 8.2.66 8.3.15	भूनाम् / भुवाम् 1.4.5 7.1.54 6.4.3 / 6.4.77
7	भुवाम् / भुवि 1.4.6 7.3.116 7.3.112 6.1.90 6.4.77 / 6.4.77	भुवोः 6.4.77 8.2.66 8.3.15	भूषु 8.3.59
भ्रू eyebrow, सुभ्रू maiden with expressive eyelashes			
Declines similar to श्री in all cases.			

स्वसृ Sister, affectionate girl

स्वसृ	स् व् अ स् ऋ = ऋकारान्तः		m
V हे	स्वसः 2.3.49 7.3.110 1.1.51 6.1.68 8.3.15	स्वसारौ	स्वसारः
1	स्वसा 7.1.94 6.4.8 6.1.68 8.2.7	स्वसारौ 7.3.110 1.1.51 6.4.11	स्वसारः 7.3.110 1.1.51 8.2.66 8.3.15
2	स्वसारम् 7.3.110 1.1.51 6.4.11	स्वसारौ 7.3.110 1.1.51 6.4.11	स्वसॄः 6.1.102 8.2.66 8.3.15
3	स्वस्रा 6.1.77	स्वसृभ्याम्	स्वसृभिः 8.2.66 8.3.15
4	स्वस्रे 6.1.77	स्वसृभ्याम्	स्वसृभ्यः 8.2.66 8.3.15
5	स्वसुः 6.1.111 8.2.24 8.3.15	स्वसृभ्याम्	स्वसृभ्यः 8.2.66 8.3.15
6	स्वसुः 6.1.111 8.2.24 8.3.15	स्वस्रोः 6.1.77 8.2.66 8.3.15	स्वसॄणाम् 7.1.54 6.4.3 8.4.2 Vartika
7	स्वसरि 7.3.110 1.1.51	स्वस्रोः 6.1.77 8.2.66 8.3.15	स्वसृषु 8.3.59
Identical to दातृ except for Accusative 2/3 where 6.1.103 didn't apply.			
By 4.1.10 stems स्वसृ तिसृ चतसृ ननान्दृ दुहितृ यातृ मातृ are not affixed with 4.1.5 ङीप् affix. These are feminine by default.			
In 1/2 1/3 2/1 2/2 3/1 4/1 6/2 7/1 7/2 we see appearance of रेफ, samprasarana equivalent of ऋकार ।			

मातृ Mother, giver of birth

मातृ	म् आ त् ऋ = ऋकारान्तः		m
V हे	मातः 2.3.49 7.3.110 1.1.51 6.1.68 8.3.15	मातरौ 7.3.110 1.1.51	मातरः 7.3.110 1.1.51 8.2.66 8.3.15
1	माता 7.1.94 6.4.8 6.1.68 8.2.7	मातरौ 7.3.110 1.1.51	मातरः 7.3.110 1.1.51 8.2.66 8.3.15
2	मातरम् 7.3.110 1.1.51	मातरौ 7.3.110 1.1.51	मातॄः 6.1.102 8.2.66 8.3.15
3	मात्रा 6.1.77	मातृभ्याम्	मातृभिः
4	मात्रे 6.1.77	मातृभ्याम्	मातृभ्यः
5	मातुः 6.1.111 1.1.51 8.2.24 8.3.15	मातृभ्याम्	मातृभ्यः
6	मातुः 6.1.111 1.1.51 8.2.24 8.3.15	मात्रोः 6.1.77 8.2.66 8.3.15	मातॄणाम् 7.1.54 6.4.3
7	मातरि 7.3.110 1.1.51	मात्रोः 6.1.77 8.2.66 8.3.15	मातृषु 8.3.59
Identical to पितृ except for 2/3 where 6.1.103 didn't apply.			
यातृ pilgrim/tourist, दुहितृ daughter, ननान्दृ husband's sister/aunt. Also other family relationships in feminine.			
By 4.1.10 stems स्वसृ तिसृ चतसृ ननान्दृ दुहितृ यातृ मातृ are not affixed with 4.1.5 ङीप् affix. These are feminine by default.			

रै Resources, Wealth

रै	र् ऐ = ऐकारान्तः		m, f
V हे	राः	रायौ	रायः
1	राः 7.2.85 8.2.66 8.3.15	रायौ 6.1.105 6.1.78	रायः 6.1.105 6.1.78 8.2.66 8.3.15
2	रायम् 6.1.78	रायौ 6.1.105 6.1.78	रायः 6.1.105 6.1.78 8.2.66 8.3.15
3	राया 6.1.78	राभ्याम् 7.2.85	राभिः 7.2.85 8.2.66 8.3.15
4	राये 6.1.78	राभ्याम् 7.2.85	राभ्यः 7.2.85 8.2.66 8.3.15
5	रायः 6.1.78 8.2.66 8.3.15	राभ्याम् 7.2.85	राभ्यः 7.2.85 8.2.66 8.3.15
6	रायः 6.1.78 8.2.66 8.3.15	रायोः 6.1.78 8.2.66 8.3.15	रायाम् 6.1.78
7	रायि 6.1.78	रायोः 6.1.78 8.2.66 8.3.15	रासु 7.2.85

This word रै is used both in masculine sense and feminine sense. The declension is as above.

गो Bull, Cow, Ox

गो	ग् ओ = ओकारान्तः		m, f
V हे	गौः	गावौ	गावः
1	गौः 7.1.90 7.2.115 8.2.66 8.3.15	गावौ 7.1.90 7.2.115 6.1.105 6.1.78	गावः 7.1.90 7.2.115 6.1.105 6.1.78 8.2.66 8.3.15
2	गाम् 6.1.93	गावौ 7.1.90 7.2.115 6.1.105 6.1.78	गाः 6.1.93 8.2.66 8.3.15
3	गवा 6.1.78	गोभ्याम्	गोभिः 8.2.66 8.3.15
4	गवे 6.1.78	गोभ्याम्	गोभ्यः 8.2.66 8.3.15
5	गोः 6.1.110 8.2.66 8.3.15	गोभ्याम्	गोभ्यः 8.2.66 8.3.15
6	गोः 6.1.110 8.2.66 8.3.15	गवोः 6.1.78 8.2.66 8.3.15	गवाम् 6.1.78
7	गवि 6.1.78	गवोः 6.1.78 8.2.66 8.3.15	गोषु 8.3.59
This word गो is used both in masculine and feminine. The declension is as above.			
Similar feminine stem द्यो = sky			

नौ Boat. ferry

नौ	न् औ = औकारान्तः		f
V हे	नौः	नावौ	नावः
1	नौः 8.2.66 8.3.15	नावौ 6.1.105 6.1.78	नावः 6.1.105 6.1.78 8.2.66 8.3.15
2	नावम् 6.1.78	नावौ 6.1.105 6.1.78	नावः 6.1.78 8.2.66 8.3.15
3	नावा 6.1.78	नौभ्याम्	नौभिः 8.2.66 8.3.15
4	नावे 6.1.78	नौभ्याम्	नौभ्यः 8.2.66 8.3.15
5	नावः 6.1.78 8.2.66 8.3.15	नौभ्याम्	नौभ्यः 8.2.66 8.3.15
6	नावः 6.1.78 8.2.66 8.3.15	नावोः 6.1.78 8.2.66 8.3.15	नावाम् 6.1.78
7	नावि 6.1.78	नावोः 6.1.78 8.2.66 8.3.15	नौषु 8.3.59

Neuter अ इ उ ऋ stem final Vowel

अजन्तः नपुंसकलिङ्गः शब्दाः wrt Maheshwar Sutras

अ , इ , उ	अ इ उ ण्	1
ऋ	ऋ ऌ क्	2
	ए ओ ङ्	3
	ऐ औ च्	4
	हयवरट्	5
	लँण्	6
	ञमङणनम्	7
	झभञ्	8
	घढधष्	9
	जबगडदश्	10
	खफछठथचटतव्	11
	कपय्	12
	शषसर्	13
	हल्	14

Note

- Diphthong ending words are only Masculine or Feminine. Neuter words do not end in ए , ऐ , ओ , औ ।
- Neuter stems decline identical to their Masculine counterparts in 3rd to 7th case.

फल fruit, natural delicacy

फल	फ् अ ल् अ	अकारान्तः	n
V हे	फल 2.3.49 7.1.24 6.1.107 6.1.69	फले	फलानि
1	फलम् 7.1.24	फले 7.1.19 6.1.87	फलानि 7.1.20 7.1.72 6.4.8
2	फलम् 7.1.24	फले 7.1.19 6.1.87	फलानि 7.1.20 7.1.72 6.4.8
3	फलेन 7.1.12 6.1.87	फलाभ्याम् 7.3.102	फलैः 7.1.9 8.2.66 6.1.88 8.3.15
4	फलाय 7.1.13 7.3.102	फलाभ्याम् 7.3.102	फलेभ्यः 7.3.103 8.2.66 8.3.15
5	फलात् 7.1.12 6.1.101	फलाभ्याम् 7.3.102	फलेभ्यः 7.3.103 8.2.66 8.3.15
6	फलस्य 7.1.12	फलयोः 7.3.104 6.1.78 8.2.66 8.3.15	फलानाम् 7.1.54 6.4.3
7	फले 6.1.87	फलयोः 7.3.104 6.1.78 8.2.66 8.3.15	फलेषु 7.3.103 8.3.59
ज्ञान knowledge, wisdom, वन forest, धन wealth, नेत्र eye			
In neuter words, the 2nd case is identical to the 1st case. All neuter words in अ decline same as राम for cases 3 to 7.			
By 2.3.49 technical term सम्बुद्धिः means Vocative 1/1			

वारि water, clear liquid

वारि	व् आ र् इ	इकारान्तः	n
V हे	वारे / वारि 7.3.108 6.1.69 / 7.1.23	वारिणी	वारीणि
1	वारि 7.1.23	वारिणी 7.1.19 7.1.73 8.4.2	वारीणि 7.1.20 7.1.73 6.4.8 8.4.2
2	वारि 7.1.23	वारिणी 7.1.19 7.1.73 8.4.2	वारीणि 7.1.20 7.1.73 6.4.8 8.4.2
3	वारिणा 7.3.120 8.4.2	वारिभ्याम्	वारिभिः 8.2.66 8.3.15
4	वारिणे 7.1.73 8.4.2	वारिभ्याम्	वारिभ्यः 8.2.66 8.3.15
5	वारिणः 7.1.73 8.2.66 8.3.15 8.4.2	वारिभ्याम्	वारिभ्यः 8.2.66 8.3.15
6	वारिणः 7.1.73 8.2.66 8.3.15 8.4.2	वारिणोः 7.1.73 8.2.66 8.3.15 8.4.2	वारीणाम् 7.1.54 6.4.3 8.4.2
7	वारिणि 7.1.73 8.4.2	वारिणोः 7.1.73 8.2.66 8.3.15 8.4.2	वारिषु 8.3.59
In neuter words, the 2nd case is identical to the 1st case.			
Neuter words ending in इ , उ , ऋ have two forms in the vocative singular V/1 because 7.3.108 and 7.1.23 apply			
3/1 form वारिणा is due to internal Sandhi from वारिना = व् आ र् इ न् आ । Here इ occurs between र् and न् hence 8.4.2 अट्कुप्वाङ्नुम्व्यवायेऽपि applies to change न् to ण् । Similarly in other forms न् is replaced by ण् ।			

दधि curd. yoghurt

दधि	द् अ ध् इ	इकारान्तः	n
V हे	दधे / दधि 7.3.108 6.1.69 / 7.1.23	दधिनी	दधीनि
1	दधि 7.1.23	दधिनी 7.1.19 7.1.73	दधीनि 7.1.20 7.1.73 6.4.8
2	दधि 7.1.23	दधिनी 7.1.19 7.1.73	दधीनि 7.1.20 7.1.73 6.4.8
3	दध्ना 7.1.75 6.4.134	दधिभ्यां	दधिभिः 8.2.66 8.3.15
4	दध्ने 7.1.75 6.4.134	दधिभ्यां	दधिभ्यः 8.2.66 8.3.15
5	दध्नः 7.1.75 6.4.134 8.2.66 8.3.15	दधिभ्यां	दधिभ्यः 8.2.66 8.3.15
6	दध्नः 7.1.75 6.4.134 8.2.66 8.3.15	दध्नोः 7.1.75 6.4.134 8.2.66 8.3.15	दध्नाम् 7.1.75 6.4.134
7	दध्नि / दधनि 7.1.75 6.4.134 / 7.1.75 6.4.136	दध्नोः 7.1.75 6.4.134 8.2.66 8.3.15	दधिषु 8.3.59
अस्थि bone, सक्थि thigh, अक्षि eye			
3rd case onwards for अजादि affixes, the इ of दधि disappears by sutra 7.1.75 अस्थि-दधि-सक्थ्यक्ष्णामनङुदात्तः ।			

शुचि pure, clean

शुचि	श् उ च् इ	इकारान्तः	n adjective
V हे	शचे / शुचि 7.3.108 6.1.69 / 7.1.23	शुचिनी	शुचीनि
1	शुचि 7.1.23	शुचिनी 7.1.19 7.1.73	शुचीनि 7.1.20 7.1.73 6.4.8
2	शुचि 7.1.23	शुचिनी 7.1.19 7.1.73	शुचीनि 7.1.20 7.1.73 6.4.8
3	शुचिना 7.3.120	शुचिभ्यां	शुचिभिः 8.2.66 8.3.15
4	शुचिने / शुचये 7.1.73 / 7.3.111 6.1.78	शुचिभ्यां	शुचिभ्यः 8.2.66 8.3.15
5	शुचिनः / शुचेः 7.1.73 8.2.66 8.3.15 / 7.3.111 6.1.110 8.2.66 8.3.15	शुचिभ्यां	शुचिभ्यः 8.2.66 8.3.15
6	शुचिनः / शुचेः 7.1.73 8.2.66 8.3.15 / 7.3.111 6.1.110 8.2.66 8.3.15	शुचिनोः / शुच्योः 7.1.73 8.2.66 8.3.15 / 6.1.77 8.2.66 8.3.15	शुचीनाम् 7.1.54 6.4.3
7	शुचिनि / शुचौ 7.1.73 / 7.3.119 6.1.88	शुचिनोः / शुच्योः 7.1.73 8.2.66 8.3.15 / 6.1.77 8.2.66 8.3.15	शुचिषु 8.3.59
अनादि having no beginning/timeless, सुरभि fragrant/sweet smell			
Template for adjectives in इ । Since adjectives can be used in all genders, hence Optional masculine forms are available.			
Notice that optional forms are same as masculine हरि			

गुरु heavy, bulky, stressful, weight bearing

गुरु	ग् उ र् उ	उकारान्तः	n adjective
V हे	गुरो / गुरु 7.3.108 6.1.69 / 7.1.23	गुरुणी	गुरूणि
1	गुरु 7.1.23	गुरुणी 7.1.19 7.1.73 8.4.2	गुरूणि 7.1.20 7.1.73 6.4.8 8.4.2
2	गुरु 7.1.23	गुरुणी 7.1.19 7.1.73 8.4.2	गुरूणि 7.1.20 7.1.73 6.4.8 8.4.2
3	गुरुणा 7.3.120 8.4.2	गुरुभ्याम्	गुरुभिः 8.2.66 8.3.15
4	गुरुणे / गुरवे 7.1.73 8.4.2 / 7.3.111 6.1.78	गुरुभ्याम्	गुरुभ्यः 8.2.66 8.3.15
5	गुरुणः / गुरोः 7.1.73 8.2.66 8.3.15 8.4.2 / 7.3.111 6.1.110 8.2.66 8.3.15	गुरुभ्याम्	गुरुभ्यः 8.2.66 8.3.15
6	गुरुणः / गुरोः 7.1.73 8.2.66 8.3.15 8.4.2 / 7.3.111 6.1.110 8.2.66 8.3.15	गुरुणोः / गुर्वोः 7.1.73 8.2.66 8.3.15 / 6.1.77 8.2.66 8.3.15	गुरूणाम् 7.1.54 6.4.3 8.4.2
7	गुरुणि / गुरौ 7.1.73 8.4.2 / 7.3.119 6.1.88	गुरुणोः / गुर्वोः 7.1.73 8.2.66 8.3.15 8.4.2 / 6.1.77 8.2.66 8.3.15	गुरुषु 8.3.59
मृदु soft, पृथु wide, पटु clever, लघु little			
Declines similar to शुचि			

Adjectives in neuter in इ, उ, ऋ e.g. शुचि, गुरु, दातृ have two forms in the singular for 4th, 5th, 6th, 7th cases, and in the dual for 6th, 7th cases. Herein notice that one form is identical to the masculine form, compare हरि, गुरु, दातृ ।

3/1 form गुरुणा is due to internal Sandhi from गुरुना = ग् उ र् उ न् आ । Here उ occurs between र् and न् hence 8.4.2 अट्कुप्वाङ्नुम्व्यवायेऽपि applies to change न् to ण् । Similarly in all other forms न् is replaced by ण् ।

मधु honey, natural sweetner

मधु	म् अ ध् उ	उकारान्तः	n
V हे	मधो / मधु 7.3.108 6.1.69 / 7.1.23	मधुनी	मधूनि
1	मधु 7.1.23	मधुनी 7.1.19 7.1.73	मधूनि 7.1.20 7.1.73 6.4.8
2	मधु 7.1.23	मधुनी 7.1.19 7.1.73	मधूनि 7.1.20 7.1.73 6.4.8
3	मधुना 7.3.120	मधुभ्याम्	मधुभिः 8.2.66 8.3.15
4	मधुने 7.1.73	मधुभ्याम्	मधुभ्यः 8.2.66 8.3.15
5	मधुनः 7.1.73 8.2.66 8.3.15	मधुभ्याम्	मधुभ्यः 8.2.66 8.3.15
6	मधुनः 7.1.73 8.2.66 8.3.15	मधुनोः 7.1.73 8.2.66 8.3.15	मधूनाम् 7.1.54 6.4.3
7	मधुनि 7.1.73	मधुनोः 7.1.73 8.2.66 8.3.15	मधुषु 8.3.59
अम्बु water, अश्रु teardrop, वस्तु thing, real thing, brahman,दारु wood			
Since this noun stem is only in neuter, hence Optional masculine forms are NOT available.			

दातृ That which gives, pot gives water

दातृ	द् आ त् ऋ	ऋकारान्तः	n adjective
V हे	दातः / दातृ 7.3.108 6.1.69 / 7.1.23	दातृणी	दातृणी
1	दातृ 7.1.23	दातृणी 7.1.19 7.1.73 8.4.2	दातॄणी 7.1.20 7.1.73 6.4.8 8.4.2
2	दातृ 7.1.23	दातृणी 7.1.19 7.1.73 8.4.2	दातॄणी 7.1.20 7.1.73 6.4.8 8.4.2
3	दातृणा / दात्रा 7.3.120 8.4.2 / 6.1.77	दातृभ्याम्	दातृभिः 8.2.66 8.3.15
4	दातृणे / दात्रे 7.1.73 8.4.2 / 6.1.77	दातृभ्याम्	दातृभ्यः 8.2.66 8.3.15
5	दातृणः / दातुः 7.1.73 8.2.66 8.3.15 8.4.2 / 6.1.111 8.2.24 8.3.15	दातृभ्याम्	दातृभ्यः 8.2.66 8.3.15
6	दातृणः / दातुः 7.1.73 8.2.66 8.3.15 8.4.2 / 6.1.111 8.2.24 8.3.15	दातृणोः / दात्रोः 7.1.73 8.2.66 8.3.15 8.4.2 / 6.1.77 8.2.66 8.3.15	दातॄणाम् 7.1.54 6.4.3 8.4.2
7	दातृणि / दातरि 7.1.73 8.4.2 / 7.3.110 1.1.51	दातृणोः / दात्रोः 7.1.73 8.2.66 8.3.15 8.4.2 / 6.1.77 8.2.66 8.3.15	दातृषु 8.3.59

कर्तृ thing that does/robotic, गन्तृ thing that moves/vehicular, वक्तृ thing that sounds/transistor radio. Adjective usage, hence optional masculine form also 3rd case onwards.

3/1 दातृ आ 7.3.120 दातृ ना 8.4.2 दातृणा । or दातृ आ 6.1.77 दात्रा ।

4/1 दातृ ए 7.1.73 दातृ न् ए 8.4.2 दातृणे । or दातृ ए 6.1.77 दात्रे ।

Masculine च् ज् त् द् न् श् ष् स् ह् stem final Consonant

हलन्तः पुंलिङ्गः प्रकरणम् wrt Maheswar Sutras and the Alphabet

	अ इ उ ण्	1	क	ख	ग	घ	ङ
	ऋ ऌ क्	2	च	छ	ज	झ	ञ
	ए ओ ङ्	3	ट	ठ	ड	ढ	ण
	ऐ औ च्	4	त	थ	द	ध	न
	हयवरट्	5	प	फ	ब	भ	म
	लँण्	6	य	र	ल	व	
न	ञमङणनम्	7	श	ष	श		
	झभञ्	8	ह				
	घढधष्	9					
ज, द	जबगडदश्	10					
च, त	खफछठथचटतव्	11					
	कपय्	12					
श, ष, स	शषसर्	13					
ह	हल्	14					

- Stems with final consonant are much easier in declension process. Especially in singular case 2/1, 3/1, 4/1, 7/1, dual case 1/2, 2/2, there isn't anything to do. Also in 5/1, 6/1, and plural case 1/3, 2/3 we only apply sutras 8.2.66, 8.3.15 for Visarga.
- Sutra 8.4.56 that gives Optional forms is not listed as such spellings are rarely seen in literature.

जलमुच् Cloud, airy ball of water

जलमुच्	च्	चकारान्तः	m	सुप् Affixes without Tag		
V हे	जलमुक्	जलमुचौ	जलमुचः	similar to case 1		
1	जलमुक् 8.2.30 6.1.68	जलमुचौ	जलमुचः 8.2.66 8.3.15	स्	औ	अस्
2	जलमुचम्	जलमुचौ	जलमुचः 8.2.66 8.3.15	अम्	औ	अस्
3	जलमुचा	जलमुग्भ्याम् 8.2.30 8.2.39	जलमुग्भिः 8.2.30 8.2.39	आ	भ्याम्	भिस्
4	जलमुचे	जलमुग्भ्याम् 8.2.30 8.2.39	जलमुग्भ्यः 8.2.30 8.2.39	ए	भ्याम्	भ्यस्
5	जलमुचः 8.2.66 8.3.15	जलमुग्भ्याम् 8.2.30 8.2.39	जलमुग्भ्यः 8.2.30 8.2.39	अस्	भ्याम्	भ्यस्
6	जलमुचः 8.2.66 8.3.15	जलमुचोः 8.2.66 8.3.15	जलमुचाम्	अस्	ओस्	आम्
7	जलमुचि	जलमुचोः 8.2.66 8.3.15	जलमुक्षु 8.2.30 8.3.59	इ	ओस्	सु
पयोमुच् cloud, सुवाच् eloquent						

1/1 जलमुच् स् 8.2.30 जलमुक् स् 6.1.68 जलमुक् ।

3/2 जलमुच् भ्याम् 8.2.30 जलमुक् भ्याम् 8.2.39 जलमुग् भ्याम् ।

7/3 जलमुच् सु 8.2.30 जलमुक् सु 8.3.59 जलमुक् षु = जलमुक्षु ।

वणिज् Merchant, trader

वणिज्	ज् = जकारान्तः		m
V हे	वणिक्	वणिजौ	वणिजः
1	वणिक् 8.2.30 8.4.55 6.1.68	वणिजौ	वणिजः 8.2.66 8.3.15
2	वणिजम्	वणिजौ	वणिजः 8.2.66 8.3.15
3	वणिजा	वणिग्भ्याम् 8.2.30	वणिग्भिः 8.2.30
4	वणिजे	वणिग्भ्याम् 8.2.30	वणिग्भ्यः 8.2.30
5	वणिजः 8.3.15 8.2.66	वणिग्भ्याम् 8.2.30	वणिग्भ्यः 8.2.30
6	वणिजः 8.3.15 8.2.66	वणिजोः 8.3.15 8.2.66	वणिजाम्
7	वणिजि	वणिजोः 8.3.15 8.2.66	वणिक्षु 8.2.30 8.4.55 8.3.59
भिषज् physician/doctor, हुतभुज् fire, ऋत्विज् priest doing havan/fire ritual			
वणिज् has same declension sutras as वाच् f			

1/1 वणिज् स् 8.2.30 वणिग् स् 8.4.55 वणिक् स् 6.1.68 वणिक् ।

3/2 वणिज् भ्याम् 8.2.30 वणिग् भ्याम् ।

7/3 वणिज् सु 8.2.30 वणिग् सु 8.4.55 वणिक् सु 8.3.59 वणिक् षु =वणिक्षु ।

राज् King, Head, President

Dhatu राज् 1cU + क्विप् → stem राज्

राज्	जकारान्तः	ज्	m
V हे	राट्	राजौ	राजः
	1	2	3
1	राट् 8.2.35 8.2.39 8.4.55 6.1.68	राजौ	राजः 8.2.66 8.3.15
2	राजम्	राजौ	राजः 8.2.66 8.3.15
3	राजा	राड्भ्याम् 8.2.35 8.2.39	राड्भिः 8.2.35 8.2.39 8.2.66 8.3.15
4	राजे	राड्भ्याम् 8.2.35 8.2.39	राड्भ्यः 8.2.35 8.2.39 8.2.66 8.3.15
5	राजः 8.2.66 8.3.15	राड्भ्याम् 8.2.35 8.2.39	राड्भ्यः 8.2.39 8.2.66 8.3.15
6	राजः 8.2.66 8.3.15	राजोः 8.2.66 8.3.15	राजाम्
7	राजि	राजोः 8.2.66 8.3.15	राट्सु 8.2.35 8.2.39 8.4.55
सम्राज् emperor, परिव्राज् ascetic, wanderer विश्वसृज् Creator, Lord			

1/1 राज् स् 8.2.35 राष् स् 8.2.39 राड् स् 8.4.55 राट् स् 6.1.68 राट् ।

Masculine stems त् ending

There are the 4 different declensions for तकारान्त masculine words as in मरुत् , पचत् , धीमत् and महत् ।

- धीमत् is Template for Dhatus to Adjectives
- पचत् is Template for शतृ / शानच् Present Participle Active Voice
- धीमत् is Template for क्तवत् Past Participle Active Voice
- पचत् is Template for क्त Past Participle Passive Voice

The feminine stems are formed with ई ending as

- पचत् = one who cooks, male पचन्ती = one who cooks, female
- धीमत् = intelligent one, male धीमती = intelligent one, female
- महत् = great one, male महती = great one, feminine

And all these feminine stems are declined as नदी

The template for PRESENT PARTICIPLE active voice

- पचत् m for masculine
- पचन्ती f for feminine (नदी)
- पचत् n for neuter (given elsewhere)

- The template for PAST PARTICIPLE active voice क्तवत्
- धीमत् m for masculine
- धीमती f for feminine (नदी)
- धीमत् n for neuter (given elsewhere)

- The template for PAST PARTICIPLE passive voice क्त(अ)

- पचतः m for masculine (राम)
- पचता f for feminine (रमा)
- पचम् n for neuter (फल)

PAST PARTICIPLE passive voice क्त ending examples

- बुद्धिमान् intelligent, धनवान् rich, कृतवान् one who has done
- भगवान् Divine, यावान् as much as, तावान् so much
- कियान् how much, इयान् to this extent, मघवान् Indra (Deva)

सत्	Root अस् 2cP = to be	त्	masculine
V हे	सन्	सन्तौ	सन्तः
1	सन्	सन्तौ	सन्तः
2	सन्तम्	सन्तौ	सतः
3	सता	सद्भ्याम्	सद्भिः
4	सते	सद्भ्याम्	सद्भ्यः
5	सतः	सद्भ्याम्	सद्भ्यः
6	सतः	सतोः	सताम्
7	सति	सतोः	सत्सु
one who is (soul), truth, to exist			
सति 7/1 = established in the one who is = सति सप्तमी clause, famous usage in Upanishad and Veda.			
Use Template पचत् ।			
3rd case onwards same as मरुत् ।			

मरुत् Wind, Hanuman, Speedy

मरुत्	तकारान्तः	त्	m	सुप् Affixes without Tag		
V हे	मरुत्	मरुतौ	मरुतः	similar to case 1		
	1	2	3	1	2	3
1	मरुत् 6.1.68 8.2.39 8.4.56	मरुतौ	मरुतः 8.2.66 8.3.15	स्	औ	अस्
2	मरुतम्	मरुतौ	मरुतः 8.2.66 8.3.15	अम्	औ	अस्
3	मरुता	मरुद्भ्याम् 8.2.39	मरुद्भिः 8.2.39 8.2.66 8.3.15	आ	भ्याम्	भिस्
4	मरुते	मरुद्भ्याम् 8.2.39	मरुद्भ्यः 8.2.39 8.2.66 8.3.15	ए	भ्याम्	भ्यस्
5	मरुतः 8.2.66 8.3.15	मरुद्भ्याम् 8.2.39	मरुद्भ्यः 8.2.39 8.2.66 8.3.15	अस्	भ्याम्	भ्यस्
6	मरुतः 8.2.66 8.3.15	मरुतोः 8.2.66 8.3.15	मरुताम्	अस्	ओस्	आम्
7	मरुति	मरुतोः 8.2.66 8.3.15	मरुत्सु	इ	ओस्	सु

1/1 मरुत् + स् → 6.1.68 → मरुत् → 8.2.39 → मरुद् → 8.4.56 → मरुत् / मरुद् । However मरुद् is not seen in literature. Only मरुत् ।

Similar Stems

भूभृत् king, इन्द्रजित् victorious over senses, कर्मकृत् businessman, विश्वजित् a specific yagya, सोमसुत् soma distiller

मरुत् is Template for

- Present participles of 3cP roots like दा – ददत् giving, दधत् holding, विभ्यत् fearing
- Present participles of 2cP roots like जक्षत् eating, जाग्रत् watching, शासत् ruling, चकासत् shining, दरिद्रत् being poor

Note – for present participles and future participles of all other parasmaipada Roots, the template is पचत् ।

पचत् Cook, Chef

पचत्	त्	तकारान्तः	m
V हे	पचन्	पचन्तौ	पचन्तः
1	पचन् 7.1.70 6.1.68 8.2.23	पचन्तौ 7.1.70 8.3.24 8.4.58	पचन्तः 7.1.70 8.3.24 8.4.58 8.2.66 8.3.15
2	पचन्तम् 7.1.70 8.3.24 8.4.58	पचन्तौ 7.1.70 8.3.24 8.4.58	पचतः 8.2.66 8.3.15
3	पचता	पचद्भ्याम् 8.2.39	पचद्भिः 8.2.39 8.2.66 8.3.15
4	पचते	पचद्भ्याम् 8.2.39	पचद्भ्यः 8.2.39 8.2.66 8.3.15
5	पचतः 8.2.66 8.3.15	पचद्भ्याम् 8.2.39	पचद्भ्यः 8.2.39 8.2.66 8.3.15
6	पचतः 8.2.66 8.3.15	पचतोः 8.2.66 8.3.15	पचताम्
7	पचति	पचतोः 8.2.66 8.3.15	पचत्सु
गच्छत्, गमिष्यत्, हरत्, हरिष्यत्, कुर्वत्, करिष्यत्, कथयत्, कथयिष्यत्			
2/3 case onwards same as मरुत्			
Template for शतृ affixed Pratipadika. Note शतृ is actually शतृँ (अत् without Tag) hence 7.1.70 applies. Dhatu + Krit affix → Pratipadika + Sup affix → Noun.			
Template for all dhatus (except for 2cP and 3cP) to make present and future participles for parasmaipada roots, in masculine.			

E.g. पच् 1cP = to cook + शतृ (अत्)

Conjugation for 1c uses शप्

पच् + शप् + अत् → no guna because absence of vowel →

पच् + अ + अत् → पच + अत् →

पररूप sandhi overrides dirgha sandhi अपदान्त अ+ गुण letter→guna letter

→ पच + अत् → पचत् (stem)

पचत् = present participle m = one who cooks = chef

पचष्यत् = future participle m = one who will cook

Declension Process

1/1 पचत् स् 7.1.70 पचत् स् 7.1.70

गम् 1cP = to go + अत्

गच्छत् = one who goes, गच्छन् going

गमिष्यत् = one who will go, गमिष्यन् willing to go

हरन् taking away, हरिष्यन् willing to take away

कुर्वन् doing, करिष्यन् willing to do

कथयन् telling, कथयिष्यन् willing to tell

धीमत् Intelligent, talented, genius

धीमत् तकारान्तः त्			adjective	मघवत्	त्	adjective
1	धीमान् 6.4.14 7.1.70 6.1.68 8.2.23	धीमन्तौ 7.1.70 8.3.24 8.4.58	धीमन्तः 7.1.70 8.3.24 8.4.58 8.2.66 8.3.15	मघवान्	मघवन्तौ	मघवन्तः
2	धीमन्तम् 7.1.70 8.3.24 8.4.58	धीमन्तौ 7.1.70 8.3.24 8.4.58	धीमतः	मघवन्तं	मघवन्तौ	मघवतः
3	धीमता	धीमद्भ्याम्	धीमद्भिः	मघवता	मघवद्भ्यां	मघवद्भिः
4	धीमते	धीमद्भ्याम्	धीमद्भ्यः	मघवते	मघवद्भ्यां	मघवद्भ्यः
5	धीमतः	धीमद्भ्याम्	धीमद्भ्यः	मघवतः	मघवद्भ्यां	मघवद्भ्यः
6	धीमतः	धीमतोः	धीमताम्	मघवततः	मघवतोः	मघवताम्
7	धीमति	धीमतोः	धीमत्सु	मघवतति	मघवतोः	मघवत्सु
V	हे धीमन्	हे धीमन्तौ	हे धीमन्तः	हे मघवन्	हेमघवन्तौ	हे मघवन्तः
Intelligent, talented, genius				cloud-like ominous, like Indra		
बुद्धिमत् , धनवत् , कृतवत् , भगवत् , यावत् , तावत् , कियत् , इयत् , विवस्वत् , मघवत् cloud-like ominous, Indra				Declines same as धीमत् , listed only for completeness.		
1/1 case, by 6.4.14 vowel becomes dirgha. शतृँ affixed Stem, hence rest SarvanamaSthana cases as पचत् । 2/3 case onwards same as मरुत् ।						

महत् Great, magnificient, noble

महत्	तकारान्तः	त्	adjective
V हे	महन्	महान्तौ	महान्तः
1	महान् 6.4.10	महान्तौ 6.4.10	महान्तः 6.4.10
2	महान्तम् 6.4.10	महान्तौ 6.4.10	महतः
3	महता	महद्भ्याम्	महद्भिः
4	महते	महद्भ्याम्	महद्भ्यः
5	महतः	महद्भ्याम्	महद्भ्यः
6	महतः	महतोः	महताम्
7	महति	महतोः	महत्सु
Not a Template for any other stem			
SarvanamaSthana cases are distinct due to 6.4.10 शतृँ affixed Stem, hence rest SarvanamaSthana cases as पचत् । 2/3 case onwards same as मरुत् ।			

सुहृद् Friend, affectionate one, good at heart

सुहृद्	दकारान्तः	द्	m
V हे	सुहृत्	सुहृदौ	सुहृदः
1	सुहृत् / सुहृद् 8.4.56	सुहृदौ	सुहृदः
2	सुहृदम्	सुहृदौ	सुहृदः
3	सुहृदा	सुहृद्भ्याम्	सुहृद्भिः
4	सुहृदे	सुहृद्भ्याम्	सुहृद्भ्यः
5	सुहृदः	सुहृद्भ्याम्	सुहृद्भ्यः
6	सुहृदः	सुहृदोः	सुहृदाम्
7	सुहृदि	सुहृदोः	सुहृत्सु 8.4.55
दिविषद् God, शास्त्रविद् well versed, तमोनुद् Sun, abolisher of darkness			
Declines identical to मरुत् except that • Sandhi 8.2.39 त् to द् is not needed here. • 1/1 by 8.4.56 we have सुहृत् / सुहृद् two Options, but only सुहृत् is seen in literature. • 7/3 सुहृद् सु 8.4.55 सुहृद् सु = सुहृत्सु ।			

सु + हृद् n = सुहृद् m = friend

हृद् n = heart

(a good heart makes a friend)

राजन् King

राजन्	नकारान्तः	न्	m
V हे	राजन् 6.1.68 8.2.8	राजानौ	राजानः
1	राजा 6.4.8 6.1.68 8.2.7 8.2.2	राजानौ 6.4.8	राजानः 6.4.8 8.2.66 8.3.15
2	राजानम् 6.4.8	राजानौ 6.4.8	राज्ञः 6.4.134 8.4.40 8.2.66 8.3.15
3	राज्ञा 6.4.134 8.4.40 8.4.44	राजभ्याम् 1.4.17 8.2.7 8.2.2	राजभिः 1.4.17 8.2.7 8.2.2 8.2.66 8.3.15
4	राज्ञे 6.4.134 8.4.40	राजभ्याम् 1.4.17 8.2.7 8.2.2	राजभ्यः 1.4.17 8.2.7 8.2.2 8.2.66 8.3.15
5	राज्ञः 6.4.134 8.4.40 8.2.66 8.3.15	राजभ्याम् 1.4.17 8.2.7 8.2.2	राजभ्यः 1.4.17 8.2.7 8.2.2 8.2.66 8.3.15
6	राज्ञः 6.4.134 8.4.40 8.2.66 8.3.15	राज्ञोः 6.4.134 8.4.40 8.2.66 8.3.15	राज्ञाम् 6.4.7 6.4.134 8.4.40 8.4.44
7	राज्ञि / राजनि 6.4.134 8.4.40 / 6.4.136	राज्ञोः 6.4.134 8.4.40 8.2.66 8.3.15	राजसु 1.4.17 8.2.7 8.2.2
मूर्धन् head, तक्षन् carpenter, सुनामन् auspiciously named, महिमन् greatness, पीवन् fat, अणिमन् minuteness, गरिमन् greatness, लघिमन् thinness			

Feminine form राज्ञी queen, declines like नदी।

आत्मन् Soul, inner purity, Jiva

आत्मन् नकारान्तः न्			m
V हे	आत्मन् 6.1.68 8.2.8	आत्मानौ	आत्मानः
1	आत्मा 6.4.8 6.1.68 8.2.7 8.2.2	आत्मानौ 6.4.8	आत्मानः 6.4.8 8.2.66 8.3.15
2	आत्मानम् 6.4.8	आत्मानौ 6.4.8	आत्मनः 6.4.137 8.2.66 8.3.15
3	आत्मना 6.4.137	आत्मभ्याम् 1.4.17 8.2.7 8.2.2	आत्मभिः 1.4.17 8.2.7 8.2.2 8.2.66 8.3.15
4	आत्मने 6.4.137	आत्मभ्याम् 1.4.17 8.2.7 8.2.2	आत्मभ्यः 1.4.17 8.2.7 8.2.2 8.2.66 8.3.15
5	आत्मनः 6.4.137 8.2.66 8.3.15	आत्मभ्याम् 1.4.17 8.2.7 8.2.2	आत्मभ्यः 1.4.17 8.2.7 8.2.2 8.2.66 8.3.15
6	आत्मनः 6.4.137 8.2.66 8.3.15	आत्मनोः 6.4.137 8.2.66 8.3.15	आत्मनाम् 6.4.7 6.4.137
7	आत्मनि 6.4.137	आत्मनोः 6.4.137 8.2.66 8.3.15	आत्मसु 1.4.17 8.2.7 8.2.2
आत्मन् is template for words ending in अन् preceded by a conjunct संयुक्ताक्षर having म् or व् for latter member e.g. त्म त्व श्व			
ब्रह्मन् Brahmin, यज्वन् Sacrificer, सुपर्वन् God, अध्वन् Way			

आत्मन् **masculine =** individual soul, the divine within each being.
ब्रह्मन् **neuter** = primal soul, undivided soul, supreme consciousness.
ब्रह्मन् **masculine** denotes a learned person, a Brahmin, or Brahma the Creator in Scriptures, but not the Supreme Consciousness.
Even the declined spellings are different.

ब्रह्मन् Brahmin the learned one, Brahma the Creator

ब्रह्मन्	नकारान्तः	न्	m
V हे	ब्रह्मन्	ब्रह्माणौ	ब्रह्माणः
1	ब्रह्मा	ब्रह्माणौ 8.4.2	ब्रह्माणः 8.4.2
2	ब्रह्माणम् 8.4.2	ब्रह्माणौ 8.4.2	ब्रह्मणः 8.4.2
3	ब्रह्मणा 8.4.2	ब्रह्मभ्याम्	ब्रह्मभिः
4	ब्रह्मणे 8.4.2	ब्रह्मभ्याम्	ब्रह्मभ्यः
5	ब्रह्मणः 8.4.2	ब्रह्मभ्याम्	ब्रह्मभ्यः
6	ब्रह्मणः 8.4.2	ब्रह्मणोः 8.4.2	ब्रह्मणाम् 8.4.2
7	ब्रह्मणि 8.4.2	ब्रह्मणोः 8.4.2	ब्रह्मसु
Declines identical to आत्मन् except that न् to ण् by 8.4.2 In Vocative singular 8.4.2 doesn't apply due to न् final.			
शर्मन् Sharma, वर्मन् Verma, some Indian Last Names			

श्वन् Dog, Canine

श्वन्	श् व् अ न्	नकारान्तः	m
V हे	श्वन्	श्वानौ	श्वानः
1	श्वा	श्वानौ	श्वानः
2	श्वानम्	श्वानौ	शुनः 6.4.133
3	शुना 6.4.133	श्वभ्याम्	श्वभिः
4	शुने 6.4.133	श्वभ्याम्	श्वभ्यः
5	शुनः 6.4.133	श्वभ्याम्	श्वभ्यः
6	शुनः 6.4.133	शुनोः 6.4.133	शुनाम् 6.4.133
7	शुनि 6.4.133	शुनोः 6.4.133	श्वसु
Declines identical to आत्मन् except for Vowel-beginning-non-SarvanamaSthana affixes. Here by 6.4.133 samprasarana वकार to उकार happens.			
Feminine form of dog is शुनी bitch, which declines like नदी			

युवन् Youth, Teenager मघवन् Storm cloud, Lord Indra

युवन्	नकारान्तः न्		m	मघवन्	न्	m
V हे	युवन्	युवानौ	युवानः	मघवन्	मघवानौ	मघवानः
1	युवा	युवानौ	युवानः	मघवा	मघवानौ	मघवानः
2	युवानम्	युवानौ	यूनः 6.4.133 6.1.101	मघवानम्	मघवानौ	मघोनः 6.4.133 6.1.87
3	यूना 6.4.133 6.1.37 6.1.108 6.1.101	युवभ्यां	युवभिः	मघोना 6.4.133 6.1.37 6.1.108 6.1.87	मघवभ्यां	मघवभिः
4	यूने 6.4.133 6.1.101	युवभ्यां	युवभ्यः	मघोने 6.4.133 6.1.87	मघवभ्यां	मघवभ्यः
5	यूनः 6.4.133 6.1.101	युवभ्यां	युवभ्यः	मघोनः 6.4.133 6.1.87	मघवभ्यां	मघवभ्यः
6	यूनः 6.4.133 6.1.101	यूनोः 6.4.133 6.1.101	यूनाम् 6.4.133 6.1.101	मघोनः 6.4.133 6.1.87	मघोनोः 6.4.133 6.1.87	मघोनाम् 6.4.133 6.1.87
7	यूनि 6.4.133 6.1.101	यूनोः 6.4.133 6.1.101	युवसु	मघोनि 6.4.133 6.1.87	मघोनोः 6.4.133 6.1.87	मघवसु
Feminine is युवति adolescent girl and declines like मति । A synonym युवती declines like नदी				Synonym मघवत् declines like धीमत्, as मघवान् । मघवन्तौ । मघवन्तः		
Declines identical to श्वन्, but 6.1.101 applies to make उ to ऊ dirgha. Rest cases like आत्मन्				Declines identical to युवन् but 6.1.87 applies. Rest cases like आत्मन्		

पथिन् Road, path, journey करिन् elephant

पथिन्	नकारान्तः न्		m	करिन्	न्	m
V हे	पन्थाः	पन्थानौ	पन्थानः	करिनः	करिणौ	करिणः
1	पन्थाः	पन्थानौ	पन्थानः	करी	करिणौ	करिणः
2	पन्थानम्	पन्थानौ	पथः	करिणम्	करिणौ	करिणः
3	पथा	पथिभ्यां	पथिभिः	करिणा	करिभ्यां	करिभिः
4	पथे	पथिभ्यां	पथिभ्यः	करिणे	करिभ्यां	करिभ्यः
5	पथः	पथिभ्यां	पथिभ्यः	करिणः	करिभ्यां	करिभ्यः
6	पथः	पथोः	पथाम्	करिणः	करिणोः	करिणाम्
7	पथि	पथोः	पथिषु	करिणि	करिणोः	करिषु
मथिन् churning handle, Mountain Meru of Purana lore.				गुणिन् good natured, धनिन् rich, शशिन् moon. Feminine forms in ई , e.g. करिणी, धनिनी decline like नदी		

2/1 form करिणम् is due to internal Sandhi from करिनम् = क् अ र् इ न् अ म् । Here इ occurs between र् and न् hence 8.4.2 अट्कुप्वाङ्नुम्व्यवायेऽपि applies to change न् to ण् । Similarly in other forms न् is replaced by ण् ।

विश् People, crowd, group of humans

विश्	शकारान्तः	श्	m
V हे	विड् / विट्	विशौ	विशः
1	विड् / विट् 6.1.68 8.2.36 8.2.39 / 8.4.56	विशौ	विशः 8.2.66 8.3.15
2	विशम्	विशौ	विशः 8.2.66 8.3.15
3	विशा	विड्भ्याम् 8.2.36 8.2.39	विड्भिः 8.2.36 8.2.39 8.2.66 8.3.15
4	विशे	विड्भ्याम् 8.2.36 8.2.39	विड्भ्यः 8.2.36 8.2.39 8.2.66 8.3.15
5	विशः 8.2.66 8.3.15	विड्भ्याम् 8.2.36 8.2.39	विड्भ्यः 8.2.36 8.2.39 8.2.66 8.3.15
6	विशः 8.2.66 8.3.15	विशोः 8.2.66 8.3.15	विशाम्
7	विशि	विशोः 8.2.66 8.3.15	विट्सु 8.2.36 8.2.39

Declension Process

3/2 विश् भ्याम् 8.2.36 → विष् भ्याम् 8.2.39 → विड् भ्याम् ।

8.2.36 says that for शकारान्त stems, श् replaced with ष् ।

8.2.39 says that an ending झल् gets जश् replacement.

झल् = row consonant letter except nasal, sibilants, aspirate

जश् = 3rd letter of every row consonant = ग् ज् ड् द् ब्

Q. What is the जश् equivalent for ष् ?

A. ष् is मूर्धा महाप्राण, ड् is मूर्धा अल्पप्राण । Rest ग् ज् द् ब् are not मूर्धा

The dhatus ending in श् like विश् 6cP = to enter, undergo change to विड् in noun form by 8.2.36 sutra since विश् → विष् and by 8.2.39 विष् → विड् ।

If followed by fullstop, 8.4.56 optionally changes विड् to विट् ।

But dhatus दिश् 6cU = to show, दृश् 1cP = to see, स्पृश् 6cP = to touch, in noun form श् changes to क् or ग् e.g. दिक् ।

तादृश् Such, like that, likewise

तादृश्	शकारान्तः	श्	adverb
V हे	तादृक्	तादृशौ	तादृशः
1	तादृक्	तादृशौ	तादृशः
2	तादृशम्	तादृशौ	तादृशः
3	तादृशा	तादृग्भ्याम्	तादृग्भिः
4	तादृशे	तादृग्भ्याम्	तादृग्भ्यः
5	तादृशः	तादृग्भ्याम्	तादृग्भ्यः
6	तादृशः	तादृशोः	तादृशाम्
7	तादृशि	तादृशोः	तादृक्षु
ईदृश् of this kind, मादृश् of my type, त्वादृश् of your type, अस्मादृश् of our type, युष्मादृश् of your type, भवादृश् of your honour's type, तत्वदृश् one who has seen the truth, experienced the Divine			
Declines similar to विश् for cases where 8.2.36 doesn't apply			

Synonym in अ e.g. तादृश (राम template)

Feminine in ई e.g. तादृशी (नदी template)

Feminine in आ e.g. ईदृशा, तादृशा (रमा template)

द्विष् Enemy, one who harbors ill-will, bitter person

द्विष्	षकारान्तः	ष्	m
V हे	द्विट्	द्विषौ	द्विषः
1	द्विट् 6.1.68 8.2.39	द्विषौ	द्विषः
2	द्विषम्	द्विषौ	द्विषः
3	द्विषा	द्विड्भ्याम् 8.2.39	द्विड्भिः 8.2.39
4	द्विषे	द्विड्भ्याम्	द्विड्भ्यः
5	द्विषः	द्विड्भ्याम्	द्विड्भ्यः
6	द्विषः	द्विषोः	द्विषाम्
7	द्विषि	द्विषोः	द्विट्सु 8.2.39
रत्नमुष् jewel thief, सितत्विष् one having white lustre			
Declines identical to विश् without need for 8.2.36			

Synonyms शत्रु , अरि ।

वेधस् all-knowledgeable, Lord Brahma, Creator

वेधस्	सकारान्तः स्		m
V हे	वेधः 6.1.68 8.2.66 8.3.15	वेधसौ	वेधसः
1	वेधाः 6.4.14 6.1.68 8.2.66 8.3.15	वेधसौ	वेधसः 8.2.66 8.3.15
2	वेधसम्	वेधसौ	वेधसः 8.2.66 8.3.15
3	वेधसा	वेधोभ्याम् 8.2.66 6.1.114 6.1.87	वेधोभिः 8.2.66 6.1.114 6.1.87 8.2.66 8.3.15
4	वेधसे	वेधोभ्याम् 8.2.66 6.1.114 6.1.87	वेधोभ्यः 8.2.66 6.1.114 6.1.87 8.2.66 8.3.15
5	वेधसः 8.2.66 8.3.15	वेधोभ्याम् 8.2.66 6.1.114 6.1.87	वेधोभ्यः 8.2.66 6.1.114 6.1.87 8.2.66 8.3.15
6	वेधसः 8.2.66 8.3.15	वेधसोः 8.2.66 8.3.15	वेधसाम्
7	वेधसि	वेधसोः 8.2.66 8.3.15	वेधस्सु / वेधःसु 8.2.66 8.3.15 8.3.34 8.3.36
चन्द्रमस् moon, सुमनस् good mind, पुरोधस् priest, मनस् mind, नचिकेतस् Nachiketas, not bowled over, undefeated			

श्रेयस् Superior, Ultimate

श्रेयस्	सकारान्तः	स्	m adjective
V हे	श्रेयन् 7.1.70 6.1.68 8.2.23	श्रेयांसौ	श्रेयांसः
1	श्रेयान् 7.1.70 6.4.10 6.1.68 8.2.23	श्रेयांसौ 7.1.70 6.4.10 8.3.24	श्रेयांसः 7.1.70 6.4.10 8.3.24 8.2.66 8.3.15
2	श्रेयांसम् 7.1.70 6.4.10 8.3.24	श्रेयांसौ 7.1.70 6.4.10 8.3.24	श्रेयसः 8.2.66 8.3.15
3	श्रेयसा	श्रेयोभ्याम् 8.2.66 6.1.114 6.1.87	श्रेयोभिः 8.2.66 6.1.114 6.1.87 8.2.66 8.3.15
4	श्रेयसे	श्रेयोभ्याम् 8.2.66 6.1.114 6.1.87	श्रेयोभ्यः 8.2.66 6.1.114 6.1.87 8.2.66 8.3.15
5	श्रेयसः 8.2.66 8.3.15	श्रेयोभ्याम् 8.2.66 6.1.114 6.1.87	श्रेयोभ्यः 8.2.66 6.1.114 6.1.87 8.2.66 8.3.15
6	श्रेयसः 8.2.66 8.3.15	श्रेयसोः 8.2.66 8.3.15	श्रेयसाम्
7	श्रेयसि	श्रेयसोः 8.2.66 8.3.15	श्रेयस्सु 8.2.66 8.3.15 8.3.34

गरीयस् heavier, स्थवीयस् greater. Feminine in ई e.g. श्रेयसी (नदी)

1/1 श्रेयस् सुँ 7.1.70 श्रेयन् स् सुँ 6.4.10 श्रेयान् स् सुँ 6.1.68 श्रेयान् स् 8.2.23 श्रेयान् ।

श्रेयस् is a stem in Taddhita ईयसुँन् affix hence 7.1.70 applies.

1/2 श्रेयस् औ 7.1.70 श्रेयन् स् औ 6.4.10 श्रेयान् स् औ 8.3.24 श्रेयां स् औ ।

By anusvara sandhi श्रेयान्सम् → श्रेयांसम् । Similarly other forms.

विद्वस् Scholar, professor

विद्वस् सकारान्तः स्			m
V हे	विद्वन् 7.1.70 6.1.68 8.2.23	विद्वांसौ	विद्वांसः
1	विद्वान् 7.1.70 6.4.10 6.1.68 8.2.23	विद्वांसौ 7.1.70 6.4.10 8.3.24	विद्वांसः 7.1.70 6.4.10 8.3.24 8.2.66 8.3.15
2	विद्वांसम् 7.1.70 6.4.10 8.3.24	विद्वांसौ 7.1.70 6.4.10 8.3.24	विदुषः 6.4.131 6.1.108 8.3.58 8.2.66 8.3.15
3	विदुषा 6.4.131 6.1.108 8.3.58	विद्वद्भ्याम् 8.2.39	विद्वद्भिः 8.2.39 8.2.66 8.3.15
4	विदुषे 6.4.131 6.1.108 8.3.58	विद्वद्भ्याम् 8.2.39	विद्वद्भ्यः 8.2.39 8.2.66 8.3.15
5	विदुषः 6.4.131 6.1.108 8.3.58 8.2.66 8.3.15	विद्वद्भ्याम् 8.2.39	विद्वद्भ्यः 8.2.39 8.2.66 8.3.15
6	विदुषः 6.4.131 6.1.108 8.3.58 8.2.66 8.3.15	विदुषोः 6.4.131 6.1.108 8.3.58 8.2.66 8.3.15	विदुषाम् 6.4.131 6.1.108 8.3.58
7	विदुषि 6.4.131 6.1.108 8.3.58	विदुषोः 6.4.131 6.1.108 8.3.58 8.2.66 8.3.15	विद्वत्सु

ऊचिवस् one who has spoken, उपेयिवस् one who has approached, सेदिवस् one who has sat, तस्थिवस् one who stood, चकृवस् one who did. Feminine in ई , e.g. विदुषी, ऊचुषी, उपेयुषी, सेदुषी, तस्थुषी ।

विद्वस् is a stem in Taddhita ईयसुँन् affix hence 7.1.70 applies. Identical to श्रेयस् for SarvanamaSthana affixes. Different 2/3 onwards. 2/3 विद्वस् अस् 6.4.131 6.1.108 विदुस् अस् 8.3.58 विदुष् अस् = विदुषस् 8.2.66 8.3.15 विदुषः । 3/2 By 8.2.39 स् changes to द् as both letters are दन्त ।

पुम्स् = पुंस् Man, male of species

पुम्स् = पुंस्	स्	m
पुमन् 7.1.70 6.1.68 8.2.23	पुमांसौ	पुमांसः
पुमान् 7.1.70 6.4.10 6.1.68 8.2.23	पुमांसौ 7.1.70 6.4.10 8.3.23	पुमांसः 7.1.70 6.4.10 8.3.23 8.2.66 8.3.15
पुमांसम् 7.1.70 6.4.10 8.3.23	पुमांसौ 7.1.70 6.4.10 8.3.23	पुंसः 8.2.66 8.3.15 8.3.23
पुंसा 8.3.23	पुंभ्याम् 1.4.18 8.2.23 8.3.23	पुंभिः 1.4.18 8.2.23 8.3.23
पुंसे 8.3.23	पुंभ्याम् 1.4.18 8.2.23 8.3.23	पुंभ्यः 1.4.18 8.2.23 8.3.23
पुंसः 8.2.66 8.3.15	पुंभ्याम् 1.4.18 8.2.23 8.3.23	पुंभ्यः 1.4.18 8.2.23 8.3.23
पुंसः 8.2.66 8.3.15	पुंसोः 8.2.66 8.3.15	पुंसाम्
पुंसि 8.3.23	पुंसोः 8.2.66 8.3.15	पुंसु 1.4.18 8.2.23 8.3.23
The Stem पुम्स् is commonly written as पुंस् by 8.3.23 anusvara sandhi.		
However for applying declension Sutras, we must use the Stem पुम्स्		
1/1 declension steps - पुम्स्+स् 7.1.70 पुम् न् स्+स् 6.4.10 पुमान् स्+स् 6.1.68 पुमान् स् 8.2.23 पुमान्		
1/2 declension steps - पुम्स्+औ 7.1.70 पुम् न् स्+औ 6.4.10 पुमान् स्+औ 8.3.23 पुमांसौ ।		
1/3 declension steps - पुम्स्+अस् = पुम्सस् 8.2.66 पुम्सर् 8.3.15 पुम्सः 8.3.23 पुंसः ।		

दोस् Arm, forearm (body part)

दोस्	सकारान्तः	स्	m
V हे	दोः	दोषौ	दोषः
1	दोः 6.1.68 8.2.66 8.3.15	दोषौ 8.3.57 8.3.58	दोषः 8.3.57 8.3.58 8.2.66 8.3.15
2	दोषम् 8.3.57 8.3.58	दोषौ 8.3.57 8.3.58	दोषः 8.3.57 8.3.58 8.2.66 8.3.15
3	दोषा 8.3.57 8.3.58	दोर्भ्याम् 8.2.66	दोर्भिः 8.2.66
4	दोषे 8.3.57 8.3.58	दोर्भ्याम् 8.2.66	दोर्भ्यः 8.2.66
5	दोषः 8.3.57 8.3.58	दोर्भ्याम् 8.2.66	दोर्भ्यः 8.2.66
6	दोषः 8.3.57 8.3.58	दोषोः 8.3.57 8.3.58 8.2.66 8.3.15	दोषाम् 8.3.57 8.3.58
7	दोषि 8.3.57 8.3.58	दोषोः 8.3.57 8.3.58 8.2.66 8.3.15	दोष्षु 8.3.57 8.3.58 8.3.59
1/2 declension steps - दोस्+औ 8.3.57 8.3.58 दोष्+औ = दोषौ ।			

लिह् One who licks, baby like, puppy like

लिह्	सकारान्तः	ह्	m
V हे	लिट्	लिहौ	लिहः
1	लिट्	लिहौ	लिहः
2	लिहम्	लिहौ	लिहः
3	लिहा	लिड्भ्याम्	लिड्भिः
4	लिहे	लिड्भ्याम्	लिड्भ्यः
5	लिहः	लिड्भ्याम्	लिड्भ्यः
6	लिहः	लिहोः	लिहाम्
7	लिहि	लिहोः	लिट्सु
भूरुह् tree, soul of earth, महीरुह् tree, soul with tall trunk			

Feminine च् ज् त् ध् न् प् भ् र् व् श् ष् स् ह् stem final Consonant

हलन्तः स्त्रीलिङ्गः प्रकरणम् wrt Maheshwar Sutras and the Alphabet

	अ इ उ ण्	1	क	ख	ग	घ	ङ
	ऋ ऌ क्	2	च	छ	ज	झ	ञ
	ए ओ ङ्	3	ट	ठ	ड	ढ	ण
	ऐ औ च्	4	त	थ	द	ध	न
व, र	हयवरट्	5	प	फ	ब	भ	म
	लँण्	6	य	र	ल	व	
न	ञमङणनम्	7	श	ष	श		
भ	झभञ्	8	ह				
ध	घढधष्	9					
ज	जबगडदश्	10					
च, त	खफछठथचटतव्	11					
प	कपय्	12					
श, ष, स	शषसर्	13					
ह	हल्	14					

Some consonant feminine stems when derived from masculine stems use the ई feminine affix and end in a vowel. These are directly declined as stem नदी f.

Generally consonant feminine stems are declined same as consonant masculine stems as per final letter.

Declension Templates for Feminine नदी , रमा

These are made from consonant ending Masculine.

Many feminine words are formed from their masculine counterparts by simply adding ई, so these become vowel ending and decline like नदी । Sutra 4.1.5 ऋन्नेभ्यो ङीप् । ङीप् = ङ् ई प् ।

Similarly, feminine words are also formed from masculine words by adding आ, so these become vowel ending and decline like रमा ।

4.1.4 अजाद्यतष्टाप् । टाप् = ट् आ प् ।

Most consonant ending feminine words are declined just the same as masculine words of appropriate ending. e.g.

feminine वाच् declines the same as masculine जलमुच् ।

feminine स्रज् declines the same as masculine वणिज् ।

feminine सरित् declines the same as masculine मरुत् ।

feminine शरद् declines the same as masculine सुहृद् ।

feminine सीमन् declines the same as masculine राजन् ।

feminine निश् declines the same as masculine विश् ।

feminine प्रावृष् declines the same as masculine द्विष् ।

वाच् Speech, Organ of speech

वाच्	चकारान्तः	च्	f	सुप् Affixes		
V हे	वाक्	वाचौ	वाचः	declension similar to 1		
	1	2	3			
1	वाक् 6.1.68 8.2.30 8.2.39 8.4.56	वाचौ	वाचः 8.2.66 8.3.15	स्	औ	अस्
2	वाचम्	वाचौ	वाचः 8.2.66 8.3.15	अम्	औ	अस्
3	वाचा	वाग्भ्याम् 8.2.30 8.2.39	वाग्भिः 8.2.30 8.2.39 8.2.66 8.3.15	आ	भ्याम्	भिस्
4	वाचे	वाग्भ्याम् 8.2.30 8.2.39	वाग्भ्यः 8.2.30 8.2.39 8.2.66 8.3.15	ए	भ्याम्	भ्यस्
5	वाचः 8.2.66 8.3.15	वाग्भ्याम् 8.2.30 8.2.39	वाग्भ्यः 8.2.30 8.2.39 8.2.66 8.3.15	अस्	भ्याम्	भ्यस्
6	वाचः 8.2.66 8.3.15	वाचोः 8.2.66 8.3.15	वाचाम्	अस्	ओस्	आम्
7	वाचि	वाचोः 8.2.66 8.3.15	वाक्षु 8.2.30 8.2.39 8.4.55 8.3.59	इ	ओस्	सु

Similar stems त्वच् skin, bark, रुच् lustre, रिच्

वाच् is identical to Template जलमुच् masculine

स्रज् garland

स्रज्	जकारान्तः	स् त् र् ज्	f
1	स्रक्	स्रजौ	स्रजः
2	स्रजम्	स्रजौ	स्रजः
3	स्रजा	स्रग्भ्यां	स्रग्भिः
4	स्रजे	स्रग्भ्यां	स्रग्भ्यः
5	स्रजः	स्रग्भ्यां	स्रग्भ्यः
6	स्रजः	स्रजोः	स्रजाम्
7	स्रजि	स्रजोः	स्रक्षु
V	हे स्रक्	हे स्रजौ	हे स्रजः
Identical to Template वणिज् m			

सरित् River, stream, Flowing current शरद् Autumn, Season

सरित्	तकारान्तः त्		f		शरद्	द्	f
V हे	सरित्	सरितौ	सरितः		हे शरत्	हे शरदौ	हे शरदः
1	सरित्	सरितौ	सरितः		शरत् / शरद् 8.4.56	शरदौ	शरदः
2	सरितम्	सरितौ	सरितः		शरतम्	शरदौ	शरदः
3	सरिता	सरिद्भ्याम्	सरिद्भिः		शरदा	शरद्भ्याम्	शरद्भिः
4	सरिते	सरिद्भ्याम्	सरिद्भ्यः		शरदे	शरद्भ्याम्	शरद्भ्यः
5	सरितः	सरिद्भ्याम्	सरिद्भ्यः		शरदः	शरद्भ्याम्	शरद्भ्यः
6	सरितः	सरितोः	सरिताम्		शरदः	शरदोः	शरदाम्
7	सरिति	सरितोः	सरित्सु		शरदि	शरदोः	शरत्सु 8.4.55
हरित् green color, तटित् lightning					सम्पद् prosperity, आपद् adversity, मृद् earth		
Sutras same as मरुत् m					Identical to सुहृद् m		
					Stem शरद् is listed as शरत् due to 8.4.55 खरि च ।		

क्षुध् Hunger, Starvation

क्षुध्	धकारान्तः	क् ष् उ ध्	f
V हे	क्षुत्	क्षुधौ	क्षुधः
1	क्षुत् 6.1.68 8.2.39 8.4.56	क्षुधौ	क्षुधः
2	क्षुधम्	क्षुधौ	क्षुधः
3	क्षुधा	क्षुद्भ्याम् 1.4.17 8.2.39	क्षुद्भिः
4	क्षुधे	क्षुद्भ्याम्	क्षुद्भ्यः
5	क्षुधः	क्षुद्भ्याम्	क्षुद्भ्यः
6	क्षुधः	क्षुधोः	क्षुधाम्
7	क्षुधि	क्षुधोः	क्षुत्सु 1.4.17 8.2.39 8.4.55

युध् war, समिध् holy wood stick for havan, mango stick for fire ritual, वीरुध् creeper. Also मर्माविध् = wounded at a marma point, = cut in a vital spot, usage as adjective in any gender declines similarly. Sutras similar to मरुत् m

1/1 declension steps -

क्षुध् +स् 6.1.68 क्षुध् 8.2.39 क्षुद् 8.4.56 क्षुद् / क्षुत् । Since क्षुत् is seen in literature we use that as the Nominative Singular form.

3/2 declension steps -

क्षुध् +भ्याम् 1.4.17 8.2.39 क्षुद् भ्याम् = क्षुद्भ्याम् ।

7/3 declension steps -

क्षुध् +सु 1.4.17 8.2.39 क्षुद् सु 8.4.55 क्षुत् सु = क्षुत्सु ।

सीमन् Boundary, limit (has two declension forms)

सीमन् नकारान्तः सुईम्अन्			f
V हे	सीमन्	सीमानौ	सीमानः
1	सीमा 4.1.11 4.1.14 6.4.143 6.4.8 6.1.68 1.4.14 8.2.7	सीमानौ 4.1.11 4.1.14 6.4.143 6.4.8	सीमानः 4.1.11 4.1.14 6.4.143 6.4.8 8.2.66 8.3.15
2	सीमानम् 4.1.11 4.1.14 6.4.143 6.4.8	सीमानौ 4.1.11 4.1.14 6.4.143 6.4.8	**सीम्नः**
3	**सीम्ना**	सीमभ्याम्	सीमभिः
4	**सीम्ने**	सीमभ्याम्	सीमभ्यः
5	**सीम्नः**	सीमभ्याम्	सीमभ्यः
6	**सीम्नः**	**सीम्नोः**	**सीम्नाम्**
7	**सीम्नि** , सीमनि	**सीम्नोः**	सीमसु
दामन् rope, garland			
See Template राजन् m. However note that in राजन् by sandhi ज्+न् अ → ज्+ञ्अ = ज्ञ । Here म्+न्अ = **म्न** ।			
Words formed above with the addition of मन् (सी+मन्) do not take the feminine termination ई though they end in न् by 4.1.11			
1/1 declension steps - सीमन् + स् 4.1.11 4.1.13 4.1.14 सीमन् स् or सीमन् डाप् स् । Steps for the form सीमन् स् । सीमन् स् 6.4.8 सीमान् स् 6.1.68 सीमान् 8.2.7 सीमा ।			

सीमन्	न्	f
सीमे	सीमे	सीमाः
सीमा	सीमे	सीमाः
सीमाम्	सीमे	सीमाः
सीमया	सीमाभ्यां	सीमाभिः
सीमायै	सीमाभ्यां	सीमाभ्यः
सीमायाः	सीमाभ्यां	सीमाभ्यः
सीमायाः	सीमयोः	सीमाणां
सीमायां	सीमयोः	सीमासु
दामन् rope, garland		
Use Template रमा f		
This is the **optional declension** for words like सीमन् , दामन् etc		
1/1 declension steps - सीमन् + स् 4.1.11 4.1.13 4.1.14 सीमन् स् or सीमन् डाप् स् । Steps for the form सीमन् डाप् स् । सीमन् डाप् स् 1.3.3 1.3.7 1.3.9 सीमन् आ स् 6.4.143 सीम् आ स् 6.1.68 सीमा ।		

अप् Waters, water sources

अप्		प्	पकारान्तः f
V	-	-	हे आपः
1	-	-	आपः 6.4.11 8.2.66 8.3.15
2	-	-	अपः 8.2.66 8.3.15
3	-	-	अद्भिः 1.4.17 7.4.48 8.2.39 8.2.66 8.3.15
4	-	-	अद्भ्यः 1.4.17 7.4.48 8.2.39 8.2.66 8.3.15
5	-	-	अद्भ्यः 1.4.17 7.4.48 8.2.39 8.2.66 8.3.15
6	-	-	अपाम्
7	-	-	अप्सु 1.4.17 8.2.39 8.4.55
Waters, saviours, purifiers			
Always in plural form only			

ककुभ् Region

ककुभ्	भकारान्तः	भ्	f
V हे	ककुप्	ककुभौ	ककुभः
1	ककुप् / ककुब् 6.1.68 8.2.39 / 8.4.56	ककुभौ	ककुभः 8.2.66 8.3.15
2	ककुभम्	ककुभौ	ककुभः 8.2.66 8.3.15
3	ककुभा	ककुब्भ्याम् 1.4.17 8.2.39 8.2.66 8.3.15	ककुब्भिः 1.4.17 8.2.39 8.2.66 8.3.15
4	ककुभे	ककुब्भ्याम् 1.4.17 8.2.39 8.2.66 8.3.15	ककुब्भ्यः 1.4.17 8.2.39 8.2.66 8.3.15
5	ककुभः 8.2.66 8.3.15	ककुब्भ्याम् 1.4.17 8.2.39 8.2.66 8.3.15	ककुब्भ्यः 1.4.17 8.2.39 8.2.66 8.3.15
6	ककुभः 8.2.66 8.3.15	ककुभोः 8.2.66 8.3.15	ककुभाम्
7	ककुभि	ककुभोः 8.2.66 8.3.15	ककुप्सु 1.4.17 8.2.39 8.4.55
Sutras same as मरुत् m			

पुर् town, city

पुर्	रेफान्तः	र्	f	सुप् Affixes		
V हे	पूः	पुरौ	पुरः	declension similar to 1		
1	पूः 6.1.68 8.2.76 8.3.15	पुरौ	पुरः 8.2.66 8.3.15	स्	औ	अस्
2	पुरम्	पुरौ	पुरः 8.2.66 8.3.15	अम्	औ	अस्
3	पुरा	पूर्भ्याम् 8.2.76 ~~8.2.77~~	पूर्भिः 8.2.76 ~~8.2.77~~ 8.2.66 8.3.15	आ	भ्याम्	भिस्
4	पुरे	पूर्भ्याम् 8.2.76 ~~8.2.77~~	पूर्भ्यः 8.2.76 ~~8.2.77~~ 8.2.66 8.3.15	ए	भ्याम्	भ्यस्
5	पुरः 8.2.66 8.3.15	पूर्भ्याम् 8.2.76 ~~8.2.77~~	पूर्भ्यः 8.2.76 ~~8.2.77~~ 8.2.66 8.3.15	अस्	भ्याम्	भ्यस्
6	पुरः 8.2.66 8.3.15	पुरोः 8.2.66 8.3.15	पुराम्	अस्	ओस्	आम्
7	पुरि	पुरोः 8.2.66 8.3.15	पूर्षु 8.2.76 ~~8.2.77~~ (8.3.16 blocks 8.3.15) 8.3.55 8.3.57 8.3.59 (8.4.48 blocks 8.4.46)	इ	ओस्	सु
Similar stems गिर् speech, धुर् yoke						

दिव् Heaven

दिव्	वकारान्तः	व्	f
V हे	द्यौः	दिवौ	दिवः
1	द्यौः	दिवौ	दिवः
2	दिवम्	दिवौ	दिवः
3	दिवा	द्युभ्याम्	द्युभिः
4	दिवे	द्युभ्याम्	द्युभ्यः
5	दिवः	द्युभ्याम्	द्युभ्यः
6	दिवः	दिवोः	दिवाम्
7	दिवि	दिवोः	द्युषु
Heaven, celestial region, area of subtle energies, world of light beings			
Nominative Singular 1/1 spelling is similar to गो m, f			

निश् Night दिश् Direction

निश्	शकारान्तः श्		f		दिश्	श्	f
V	हे निट्	हे निशौ	हे निशः		हे दिक्	हे दिशौ	हे दिशः
1	निट्	निशौ	निशः		दिक्	दिशौ	दिशः
2	निशम्	निशौ	निशः		दिशम्	दिशौ	दिशः
3	निशा	निड्भ्याम्	निड्भिः		दिशा	दिग्भ्याम्	दिग्भिः
4	निशे	निड्भ्याम्	विड्भ्यः		दिशे	दिग्भ्याम्	दिग्भ्यः
5	निशः	निड्भ्याम्	निड्भ्यः		दिशः	दिग्भ्याम्	दिग्भ्यः
6	निशः	निशोः	निशाम्		दिशः	दिशोः	दिशाम्
7	निशि	निशोः	निट्सु		दिशि	दिशोः	दिक्षु
विपाश् beas river in punjab					e.g. east, south west		
Use Template विश् m					Use Template तादृश् m		
Synonym निशा f declines like रमा, निशा । निशे । निशाः ।					Synonym ककुभ् f		

Notes – By Sandhi

The ending श् of dhatu-nouns (dhatus that form nouns) is changed to ट् or ड् (note that निश् is a noun). But the ending श् of dhatus (dhatus that form verbs) is changed to क् or ग् ।

प्रावृष् Rainy season, Monsoon

प्रावृष्	षकारान्तः	ष्	f
V हे	प्रावृट्	प्रावृषौ	प्रावृषः
1	प्रावृट्	प्रावृषौ	प्रावृषः
2	प्रावृषम्	प्रावृषौ	प्रावृषः
3	प्रावृषा	प्रावृड्भ्याम्	प्रावृड्भिः
4	प्रावृषे	प्रावृड्भ्याम्	प्रावृड्भ्यः
5	प्रावृषः	प्रावृड्भ्याम्	प्रावृड्भ्यः
6	प्रावृषः	प्रावृषोः	प्रावृषाम्
7	प्रावृषि	प्रावृषोः	प्रावृट्सु
similar त्विष् lustre			
Use Template द्विष् m			
प्रावृष् has same declension sutras as राज् m			

भास् Light, illumination, understanding आशिस् Blessing, grace

भास्	सकारान्तः स्		f	आशिस्	स्	f
V हे	भाः	भासौ	भासः	आशीः	आशिषौ	आशिषः
1	भाः	भासौ	भासः	आशीः	आशिषौ	आशिषः
2	भासम्	भासौ	भासः	आशिषम्	आशिषौ	आशिषः
3	भासा	भाभ्यां	भाभिः	आशिषा	आशीर्भ्यां	आशीर्भिः
4	भासे	भाभ्यां	भाभ्यः	आशिषे	आशीर्भ्यां	आशीर्भ्यः
5	भासः	भाभ्यां	भाभ्यः	आशिषः	आशीर्भ्यां	आशीर्भ्यः
6	भासः	भासोः	भासाम्	आशिषः	आशिषोः	आशिषाम्
7	भासि	भासोः	भास्सु	आशिषि	आशिषोः	आशिष्षु
उषस् dawn						

उपानह् Shoe, Belly

उपानह्	हकारान्तः	ह्	f
V हे	उपानत्	उपानहौ	उपानहः
1	उपानत्	उपानहौ	उपानहः
2	उपानहम्	उपानहौ	उपानहः
3	उपानहा	उपानद्भ्याम्	उपानद्भिः
4	उपानहे	उपानद्भ्याम्	उपानद्भ्यः
5	उपानहः	उपानद्भ्याम्	उपानद्भ्यः
6	उपानहः	उपानहोः	उपानहाम्
7	उपानहि	उपानहोः	उपानत्सु
Shoe (sandals), boots, alter ego			

Neuter च् ज् त् द् न् श् ष् स् ह् stem final Consonant

हलन्तः नपुंसकलिङ्ग प्रकरणम् wrt Maheswar Sutras and the Alphabet

	अ इ उ ण्	1	क	ख	ग	घ	ङ
	ऋ ऌ क्	2	च	छ	ज	झ	ञ
	ए ओ ङ्	3	ट	ठ	ड	ढ	ण
	ऐ औ च्	4	त	थ	द	ध	न
र	हयवरट्	5	प	फ	ब	भ	म
	लँण्	6	य	र	ल	व	
न	ञमङणनम्	7	श	ष	श		
	झभञ्	8	ह				
	घढधष्	9					
ज, द	जबगडदश्	10					
च, त	खफछठथचटतव्	11					
	कपय्	12					
श, ष, स	शषसर्	13					
ह	हल्	14					

Most consonant ending neuter words are declined just the same as masculine words of appropriate ending, case 3 onwards.

सुवाच् Eloquent speech, oratory

सुवाच्	चकारान्तः	च्	n
V हे	सुवाक्	सुवाची	सुवाञ्चि
1	सुवाक् / सुवाग् 7.1.23 1.4.17 8.2.30 8.2.39 / 8.4.56	सुवाची 7.1.19	सुवाञ्चि 7.1.20 7.1.72 8.3.24 8.4.58
2	सुवाक् 7.1.23 1.4.17 8.2.30 8.2.39 8.4.56	सुवाची 7.1.19	सुवाञ्चि 7.1.20 7.1.72 8.3.24 8.4.58
3	सुवाचा	सुवाग्भ्याम् 1.4.17 8.2.30 8.2.39	सुवाग्भिः 1.4.17 8.2.30 8.2.39 8.2.66 8.3.15
4	सुवाचे	सुवाग्भ्याम् 1.4.17 8.2.30 8.2.39	सुवाग्भ्यः 1.4.17 8.2.30 8.2.39 8.2.66 8.3.15
5	सुवाचः 8.2.66 8.3.15	सुवाग्भ्याम् 1.4.17 8.2.30 8.2.39	सुवाग्भ्यः 1.4.17 8.2.30 8.2.39 8.2.66 8.3.15
6	सुवाचः 8.2.66 8.3.15	सुवाचोः 8.2.66 8.3.15	सुवाचाम्
7	सुवाचि	सुवाचोः 8.2.66 8.3.15	सुवाक्षु 8.2.30 8.3.59
Template जलमुच् m (3rd case onwards)			

Notice that the upasarga सु + वाच् f made it सुवाच् neuter

असृज्

असृज्	जकारान्तः	ज्	n
V हे	असृक्	असृजी	असृञ्जि
1	असृक्	असृजी	असृञ्जि
2	असृक्	असृजी	असृञ्जि
3	असृजा	असृग्भ्यां	असृग्भिः
4	असृजे	असृग्भ्यां	असृग्भ्यः
5	असृजः	असृग्भ्यां	असृग्भ्यः
6	असृजः	असृजोः	असृजाम्
7	असृजि	असृजोः	असृक्षु
blood			
Template वणिज् m (3rd case onwards)			

जगत् world, society

जगत्	तकारान्तः	त्	n
1	जगत्	जगती	जगन्ति
2	जगत्	जगती	जगन्ति
3	जगता	जगद्भ्याम्	जगद्भिः
4	जगते	जगद्भ्याम्	जगद्भ्यः
5	जगतः	जगद्भ्याम्	जगद्भ्यः
6	जगतः	जगतोः	जगताम्
7	जगति	जगतोः	जगत्सु
V	हे जगत्	हे जगती	हे जगन्ति
World (manifest creation), universe, conglomerate of name and form			
भास्वत् shining, गतवत् one who went, सुन्वत् extracting, तन्वत् stretching, रुन्धत् preventing, क्रीणत् buying, अदत् eating, बृहत् great, पृषत् waterdrop			
Template मरुत् m (3rd case onwards)			
जगत् is template for many neuter words			

मत्वन्ताः , वत्वन्ताः , etc. present participle active शतृ ending (roots of conjugations स्वादि 5c, तनादि 7c, रुधादि 8c, and क्रयादि 9c)

ददत् act of giving charity तुदत् act of giving pain

ददत्	तकारान्तः त्		n participle		तुदत्	त्	n participle
V हे	ददत्	ददती	ददति , ददन्ति		तुदत्	तुदन्ती , तुदती	तुदन्ति
1	ददत्	ददती	ददति , ददन्ति		तुदत्	तुदन्ती , तुदती	तुदन्ति
2	ददत्	ददती	ददति , ददन्ति		तुदत्	तुदन्ती , तुदती	तुदन्ति
3	ददता	ददद्भ्यां	ददद्भिः		तुदता	तुदद्भ्यां	तुदद्भिः
4	ददते	ददद्भ्यां	ददद्भ्यः		तुदते	तुदद्भ्यां	तुदद्भ्यः
5	ददतः	ददद्भ्यां	ददद्भ्यः		तुदतः	तुदद्भ्यां	तुदद्भ्यः
6	ददतः	ददतोः	ददताम्		तुदतः	तुदतोः	तुदताम्
7	ददति	ददतोः	ददत्सु		तुदति	तुदतोः	तुदत्सु
Giving (the act of, to give), Active present participle verb-noun. From 3c Root दा					Giving pain (the act of) Active present participle verb-noun. From 6c Root तुद्		
जुह्वत् sacrificing, शंसत् ruling, जक्षत् eating, चकासत् shining,दरिद्रत् one becoming poor,जाग्रत् being awake					पृच्छत् asking, मुञ्चत् releasing, यात् going, भात् shining, करिष्यत् one who will do		
Template मरुत् m (3rd case onwards)					Template मरुत् m (3rd case onwards)		

पचत् act of cooking

पचत्	तकारान्तः	त्	n participle
V हे	पचत्	पचन्ती	पचन्ति
1	पचत्	पचन्ती	पचन्ति
2	पचत्	पचन्ती	पचन्ति
3	पचता	पचद्भ्याम्	पचद्भिः
4	पचते	पचद्भ्याम्	पचद्भ्यः
5	पचतः	पचद्भ्याम्	पचद्भ्यः
6	पचतः	पचतोः	पचताम्
7	पचति	पचतोः	पचत्सु
cooking (the act of), Active present participle verb-noun. From 1c Root पच्			
भवत् being, दीव्यत् playing, चोरयत् stealing, चिकीर्षत् desiring to do, पुत्रीयत् desiring a child			
Template मरुत् m (3rd case onwards)			
Compare with masculine पचत्			
पचत् is Template for neuter present participles active voice शतृ कर्त्तरि प्रयोगः ।			

महत् massive, huge, great

महत्	तकारान्तः	त्	n
V हे	महत्	महती	महान्ति
1	महत्	महती	महान्ति
2	महत्	महती	महान्ति
3	महता	महद्भ्याम्	महद्भिः
4	महते	महद्भ्याम्	महद्भ्यः
5	महतः	महद्भ्याम्	महद्भ्यः
6	महतः	महतोः	महताम्
7	महति	महतोः	महत्सु
Compare with masculine महत्			
Template मरुत् m (3rd case onwards)			

हृद् heart, core, blueprint of something

हृद्	दकारान्तः	द्	n
V हे	हृत्	हृदी	हृन्दि
1	हृत्	हृदी	हृन्दि
2	हृत्	हृदी	हृन्दि
3	हृदा	हृद्भ्याम्	हृद्भिः
4	हृदे	हृद्भ्याम्	हृद्भ्यः
5	हृदः	हृद्भ्याम्	हृद्भ्यः
6	हृदः	हृदोः	हृदाम्
7	हृदि	हृदोः	हृत्सु
Compare with masculine सुहृद्			
Template सुहृद् m (3rd case onwards)			

नामन् name, surname, formal name, label

नामन्	नकारान्तः	न्	n
V हे	नामन् , नाम	नाम्नी , नामनी	नामानि
1	नाम	नाम्नी , नामनी	नामानि
2	नाम	नाम्नी , नामनी	नामानि
3	नाम्ना	नामभ्याम्	नामभिः
4	नाम्ने	नामभ्याम्	नामभ्यः
5	नाम्नः	नामभ्याम्	नामभ्यः
6	नाम्नः	नाम्नोः	नाम्नाम्
7	नाम्नि , नामनि	नाम्नोः	नामसु
धामन् lustre, house, व्योमन् sky, हेमन् gold			
Template राजन् m (3rd case onwards). However note that in राजन् forms, by sandhi ज् + न् = ज् + ञ् = ज्ञ । That does not occur here. म् + न् = म्न ।			

कर्मन् action ब्रह्मन् supreme consciousness

कर्मन् नकारान्तः न्			n	ब्रह्मन्	न्	n
V हे	कर्मन् , कर्म	कर्मणी	कर्मणि	ब्रह्मन् , ब्रह्म	ब्रह्मणी	ब्रह्मणि
1	कर्म	कर्मणी	कर्मणि	ब्रह्म	ब्रह्मणी	ब्रह्मणि
2	कर्म	कर्मणी	कर्मणि	ब्रह्म	ब्रह्मणी	ब्रह्मणि
3	कर्मणा	कर्मभ्यां	कर्मभिः	ब्रह्मणा	ब्रह्मभ्यां	ब्रह्मभिः
4	कर्मणे	कर्मभ्यां	कर्मभ्यः	ब्रह्मणे	ब्रह्मभ्यां	ब्रह्मभ्यः
5	कर्मणः	कर्मभ्यां	कर्मभ्यः	ब्रह्मणः	ब्रह्मभ्यां	ब्रह्मभ्यः
6	कर्मणः	कर्मनोः	कर्मनां	ब्रह्मणः	ब्रह्मनोः	ब्रह्मनां
7	कर्मणि	कर्मनोः	कर्मसु	ब्रह्मणि	ब्रह्मनोः	ब्रह्मसु
Action, physical or mental work				Primal soul, supreme consciousness, ultimate reality of scriptures		
ब्रह्मन् soul, जन्मन् birth, शर्मन् happiness, वर्मन् armour, वेश्मन् house, सद्मन् house				declines same as कर्मन्		
Template आत्मन् m (3rd case onwards)				Template ब्रह्मन् m (3rd case onwards)		

अहन् day (duration between 6am to 6pm)

अहन्	नकारान्तः न्		n
V हे	अहः	अह्नी , अहनी	अहानि
1	अहः	अह्नी , अहनी	अहानि
2	अहः	अह्नी , अहनी	अहानि
3	अह्ना	अहोभ्याम्	अहोभिः
4	अह्ने	अहोभ्याम्	अहोभ्यः
5	अह्नः	अहोभ्याम्	अहोभ्यः
6	अह्नः	अह्नोः	अह्नाम्
7	अह्नि , अहनि	अह्नोः	अहस्सु
Day, the 24-hour span			
A rare neuter declension that does not have a corresponding masculine template			
Pronounce अह्न as अनः (अनह aspirated – **anh** rather than ***ahn***). This is one of the rare words in Sanskrit that is not pronounced as it is written!			

गुणिन् meritorious

गुणिन्	नकारान्तः	न्	n adjective
V हे	गुणिन् , गुणि	गुणिनी	गुणीनि
1	गुणि	गुणिनी	गुणीनि
2	गुणि	गुणिनी	गुणीनि
3	गुणिना	गुणिभ्यां	गुणिभिः
4	गुणिने	गुणिभ्यां	गुणिभ्यः
5	गुणिनः	गुणिभ्यां	गुणिभ्यः
6	गुणिनः	गुणिणोः	गुणिणाम्
7	गुणिनि	गुणिणोः	गुणिषु
कुशलिन् happy, वाग्मिन् orator, दण्डिन् one having a stick (Dandiswami)			
Template करिन् m (3rd case onwards)			

वार् water, still waters, deep blue sea

वार्	रेफान्तः	र्	n
V हे	वाः	वारी	वारि
1	वाः	वारी	वारि
2	वाः	वारी	वारि
3	वारा	वार्भ्यां	वार्भिः
4	वारे	वार्भ्यां	वार्भ्यः
5	वारः	वार्भ्यां	वार्भ्यः
6	वारः	वरोः	वराम्
7	वारि	वरोः	वार्षु
Synonym वारी n , Template गिर् f (3rd case onwards)			

तादृश् likewise

तादृश्	शकारान्तः	श्	n adverb
V हे	तादृक्	तादृशी	तादृंशि
1	तादृक्	तादृशी	तादृंशि
2	तादृक्	तादृशी	तादृंशि
3	तादृशा	तादृग्भ्याम्	तादृग्भिः
4	तादृशे	तादृग्भ्याम्	तादृग्भ्यः
5	तादृशः	तादृग्भ्याम्	तादृग्भ्यः
6	तादृशः	तादृशोः	तादृशाम्
7	तादृशि	तादृशोः	तादृक्षु
Such, like (like that, of that kind)			
ईदृश् of this kind, एतादृश् of this kind, कीदृश् of what kind?			
Template तादृश् m (3rd case onwards) By anusvara sandhi तादृन्शि to तादृंशि ।			

सुत्विष् shiny, glowing, lustrous

सुत्विष्	षकारान्तः	ष्	n adjective
V हे	सुत्विट्	सुत्विषी	सुत्वींषि
1	सुत्विट्	सुत्विषी	सुत्वींषि
2	सुत्विट्	सुत्विषी	सुत्वींषि
3	सुत्विषा	सुत्विड्भ्याम्	सुत्विड्भिः
4	सुत्विषे	सुत्विड्भ्याम्	सुत्विड्भ्यः
5	सुत्विषः	सुत्विड्भ्याम्	सुत्विड्भ्यः
6	सुत्विषः	सुत्विषोः	सुत्विषाम्
7	सुत्विषि	सुत्विषोः	सुत्विट्सु
Lustrous (glowing), brilliant			
रत्नमुष् jewel thief, usually this is masculine; however if an animal or bird tries to steal something sparkling, it gets a neuter connotation.			
Template द्विष् m (3rd case onwards)			

By anusvara sandhi सुत्वीन्षि to सुत्वींषि ।

मनस् mind, thoughts, opinion हविस् Oblation

मनस्	सकारान्तः स्		n	हविस्	स्	n
V हे	मनः	मनसी	मनांसि	हविः	हविषी	हवींषि
1	मनः	मनसी	मनांसि	हविः	हविषी	हवींषि
2	मनः	मनसी	मनांसि	हविः	हविषी	हवींषि
3	मनसा	मनोभ्यां	मनोभिः	हविषा	हविर्भ्यां	हविर्भिः
4	मनसे	मनोभ्यां	मनोभ्यः	हविषे	हविर्भ्यां	हविर्भ्यः
5	मनसः	मनोभ्यां	मनोभ्यः	हविषः	हविर्भ्यां	हविर्भ्यः
6	मनसः	मनसोः	मनसाम्	हविषः	हविषोः	हविषाम्
7	मनसि	मनसोः	मनस्सु	हविषि	हविषोः	हविष्षु
Mind, the thought machine, opinion				Oblation, offering of ghee into a fire ritual		
तपस् penance, यशस् fame, गरीयस् heavier, श्रेयस् best, तमस् ignorance				सर्पिस् ghee, ज्योतिस् light, glow, रोचिस् light		
Template वेधस् m (3rd case onwards)				Neuter that doesn’t have corresponding masculine template		
Any words ending in ईयस् e.g. गरीयस् , अपि also क्लीबे in neuter एवमेव । decline like this only.						

By anusvara sandhi मनान्सि to मनांसि । हवीन्षि to हवींषि । 8.3.24 नश्चापदान्तस्य झलि ।

वपुस् body, trunk तस्थिवस् that which stands steadfast, pillar

वपुस्	सकारान्तः स्		n	तस्थिवस्	तस् थि वस्	n
V हे	वपुः	वपुषी	वपूंषि	तस्थिवत्	तस्थुषी	तस्थिवांसि
1	वपुः	वपुषी	वपूंषि	तस्थिवत्	तस्थुषी	तस्थिवांसि
2	वपुः	वपुषी	वपूंषि	तस्थिवत्	तस्थुषी	तस्थिवांसि
3	वपुषा	वपुर्भ्यां	वपुर्भिः	तस्थुषा	तस्थिवद्भ्यां	तस्थिवद्भिः
4	वपुषे	वपुर्भ्यां	वपुर्भ्यः	तस्थुषे	तस्थिवद्भ्यां	तस्थिवद्भ्यः
5	वपुषः	वपुर्भ्यां	वपुर्भ्यः	तस्थुषः	तस्थिवद्भ्यां	तस्थिवद्भ्यः
6	वपुषः	वपुषोः	वपुषाम्	तस्थुषः	तस्थुषोः	तस्थुषाम्
7	वपुषि	वपुषोः	वपुष्षु	तस्थुषि	तस्थुषोः	तस्थिवत्सु

body	That which has stood (one who has stood)
आयुस् life, चक्षुस् eye, धनुस् bow	ऊचिवस् that which has spoken, उपेयिवस् that which has approached
Synonym शरीर m	
Declines same as हविस् n	Template विद्वस् m (3rd case onwards)

By anusvara sandhi वपून्षि to वपूंषि । 8.3.24 नश्चापदान्तस्य झलि । Appearance of षकार by consonant sandhi 8.3.55 अपदान्तस्य मूर्धन्यः । 8.3.57 इण्कोः । 8.3.59 आदेशप्रत्यययोः । वप्+उ+स्+अजादि सुप् -> वप्+उ+ष्+अजादि सुप् ।

अम्भोरुह् lotus, flower that grows in water

अम्भोरुह्	हकारान्तः	ह्	n
V हे	अम्भोरुट्	अम्भोरुही	अम्भोरुंहि
1	अम्भोरुट् / ड्	अम्भोरुही	अम्भोरुंहि
2	अम्भोरुट् / ड्	अम्भोरुही	अम्भोरुंहि
3	अम्भोरुहा	अम्भोरुड्भ्याम्	अम्भोरुड्भिः
4	अम्भोरुहे	अम्भोरुड्भ्याम्	अम्भोरुड्भ्यः
5	अम्भोरुहः	अम्भोरुड्भ्याम्	अम्भोरुड्भ्यः
6	अम्भोरुहः	अम्भोरुहोः	अम्भोरुहाम्
7	अम्भोरुहि	अम्भोरुहोः	अम्भोरुट्सु
Lotus, the soul of water			
Template लिह् m (3rd case onwards)			

By anusvara sandhi अम्भोरुन्हि to अम्भोरुंहि ।

॥ इति हलन्त नपुंसकलिङ्ग प्रकरणम् ॥

॥ इति हलन्त प्रकरणम् ॥

॥ इति साधारणशब्द विभागः ॥

This ends the declined forms of general regular declined words.

Sarvanama (35 Pronoun Stems in Ganapatha)

The Sanskrit word for Pronoun is सर्व-नाम = Any-Name, i.e. that which refers to any नाम = Noun.
Grammatically, सर्वनाम refers to a collection of Stems that have specific declension Sutras. Most of these stems are used as pronouns, whereas a few are general nouns.

There are some 35 pronoun stems classified under 6 types:
1. Personal Pronouns - स्व युष्मद् अस्मद् भवत् oneself you, I, your honor,
2. Relative Pronouns – यद् यतर यतम (+डतर +डतम) that, which
3. Interrogative Pronouns – किम् (कतर कतम) who, what
4. Demonstrative Pronouns – सर्व विश्व अन्य अन्यतर इतर त्वत् त्व नेम सम सिम त्यद् तद् एतद् इदम् अदस् (ततर ततम) this, that
5. Numeral Pronouns – एक द्वि उभ उभय a, two, both, both side
6. Directional Pronouns – पूर्व पर अवर दक्षिण उत्तर अपर अध अन्तर inner, eastern, outer

Notes regarding the Pronoun Stems
- There is no Vocative case for personal pronouns
- There is a word with same spelling **अन्यतम** but is not a pronoun, and that declines like **राम** m
- **सम** when it means 'all' is a pronoun and declines accordingly, when it means 'equal to' it declines like **राम** m
- Relative distances of demonstrative pronouns
    - इदम् closest, e.g. my body
    - एतद् close, e.g. my dress
    - अदस् distant, e.g. the fan
    - तद् far away, not seen, e.g. beyond yonder hill

Pronoun Stems & Sutras

1.1.27 **सर्वादीनि सर्वनामानि ।**

It points to the ganapatha which lists the 35 Sarvanama stems.
सर्व विश्व उभ उभय डतर डतम अन्य अन्यतर इतर त्वत् त्व नेम सम सिम ।
पूर्व पर अवर दक्षिण उत्तर अपर अध ।
स्व(म्) ।
अन्तर(म्) ।
त्यद् तद् यद् एतद् इदम् अदस् एक द्वि युष्मद् अस्मद् भवत्(उँ) किम् ।

- 23 अकारान्त Stems सर्व विश्व उभ उभय डतर डतम अन्य अन्यतर इतर त्व नेम सम सिम पूर्व पर अवर दक्षिण उत्तर अपर अध स्व अन्तर एक
- 1 इकारान्त Stem द्वि
- 8 तकारान्त Stems त्वत् त्यद् तद् यद् एतद् युष्मद् अस्मद् भवत्
- 2 मकारान्त Stems इदम् किम्
- 1 सकारान्त Stem अदस्

Note

डतर डतम are not stems, rather the किम् यत् तद् 3x2 = 6 stems ending in these affixes, कतर कतम यतर यतम ततर ततम ।

Thus the Pronoun stems are actually 39 in all.

Note

Pronoun Stems can be used as adjectives in all three genders mfn, so decline corresponding to their mfn counterparts.

Pronoun Gender Stems

SN	Ganapatha	Masculine	Feminine	Neuter
1	सर्व	सर्व	सर्वा	सर्व
2	विश्व	विश्व	विश्वा	विश्व
3	उभ	उभ	उभा	उभ
4	उभय	उभय	उभयी	उभय
5	किम्+डतर	कतर	कतरा	कतर
6	किम्+डतम	कतम	कतमा	कतम
7	अन्य	अन्य	अन्या	अन्य
8	अन्यतर	अन्यतर	अन्यतरा	अन्यतर
9	इतर	इतर	इतरा	इतर
10	त्वत्	त्वत्	त्वत्	त्वत्
11	त्व	त्व	त्वा	त्व
12	नेम	नेम	नेमा	नेम
13	सम	सम	समा	सम
14	सिम	सिम	सिमा	सिम
15	पूर्व	पूर्व	पूर्वा	पूर्व
16	पर	पर	परा	पर
17	अवर	अवर	अवरा	अवर
18	दक्षिण	दक्षिण	दक्षिणा	दक्षिण
19	उत्तर	उत्तर	उत्तरा	उत्तर
20	अपर	अपर	अपरा	अपर
21	अध	अध	अधा	अध
22	स्व	स्व	स्वा	स्व
23	अन्तर	अन्तर	अन्तरा	अन्तर
24	त्यद्	त्यद्	त्यद्	त्यद्

25	तद्	तद्	तद्	तद्
26	यद्	यद्	यद्	यद्
27	एतद्	एतद्	एतद्	एतद्
28	इदम्	इदम्	इदम्	इदम्
29	अदस्	अदस्	अदस्	अदस्
30	एक	एक	एका	एक
31	द्वि	द्व	द्वा	द्व
32	युष्मद्	युष्मद्	युष्मद्	युष्मद्
33	अस्मद्	अस्मद्	अस्मद्	अस्मद्
34	भवत्	भवत्	भवती	भवत्
35	किम्	क	का	कि
36	यद्+डतर	यतर	यतरा	यतर
37	यद्+डतम	यतम	यतमा	यतम
38	तत्+डतर	ततर	ततरा	ततर
39	तत्+डतम	ततम	ततमा	ततम

Following stems decline identically

- सर्व विश्व अन्य अन्यतर इतर त्व सम सिम, डतर डतम affixed - कतर कतम यतर यतम ततर ततम, एक Pronoun declension sutras apply when used in sense of “a/the”
- डतर डतम affixed कतर कतम यतर यतम ततर ततम neuter are तकारान्त for nominative & accusative singular case
- उभ
- उभय
- नेम

- पूर्व पर अवर दक्षिण उत्तर अपर अध स्व अन्तर (Pronoun declension Sutras apply in specific usage, and are also declined as regular nouns otherwise)

Principal Sutras for अ-ending Stems

7.1.14 सर्वनाम्नः स्मै । Affix ङे 4/1 replaced by स्मै ।
7.1.15 ङसिङ्योः स्मात्स्मिनौ । Affix ङसिँ 5/1 replaced by स्मात् , Affix ङस् 6/1 replaced by स्मिन् ।
7.1.16 पूर्वादिभ्यो नवभ्यो वा । Affix ङसिँ 5/1 replaced by स्मात् , Affix ङि 7/1 replaced by स्मिन् , for the पूर्वादि nine stems, Optionally.
7.1.17 जसः शी । The जस् 1/3 affix is replaced by शी = श् ई ।
7.1.52 आमि सर्वनाम्नः सुट् । Augment स् applies for आम् 6/3 affix.

Sutras that affect declension of listed Sarvanama Stems

1.1.33 प्रथमचरमतयाल्पार्धकतिपय-नेम(ाः) च ।
1.1.34 पूर्व-पर-अवर-दक्षिण-उत्तर-अपर-अध(राणि) व्यवस्थायाम् असंज्ञायाम् ।
1.1.35 स्व-म् अज्ञाति-धन-आख्यायाम् । Pronoun declension sutras apply when this is NOT used in the sense of genus/worth (i.e. when it used in the sense of "oneself").
1.1.36 अन्तर-म् बहिर्योगोपसंव्यानयोः । Pronoun declension sutras apply when it is used in the sense of "an outer layer that is closest".

Sutras that affect declension due to specific Usage

2.3.27 सर्वनाम्नस्तृतीया च ।
5.3.2 किंसर्वनामबहुभ्योऽद्व्यादिभ्यः ।
5.3.71 अव्ययसर्वनाम्नामकच् प्राक् टेः ।
5.3.92 किंयत्तदो निर्द्धारणे द्वयोरेकस्य डतरच् ।
5.3.93 वा बहूनां जातिपरिप्रश्ने डतमच् ।

5.3.94 एकाच्च प्राचाम् ।

6.3.91 आ सर्वनाम्नः ।

7.3.114 सर्वनाम्नः स्याड्ढ्रस्वश्च ।

Sutras for Sarvanama-Sthana Affixes

1.1.42 शि सर्वनामस्थानम् । affix शि gets सर्वनामस्थानम् technical name.

7.1.20 जश्शसोः शिः । the 1/3 affix जस् and 2/3 affix शस् are replaced by शि for neuter stems.

1.4.17 सुँ-आदिषु अ-सर्वनामस्थाने । the initial five affixes सुँ औ जस् अम् औट् are सर्वनामस्थानम् for non-neuter stems.

6.1.70 शेश्छन्दसि बहुलम् । affix शि is used arbitrarily in Vedas.

6.1.170 अञ्चेश्छन्दसि अ-सर्वनामस्थानम् ।

6.1.199 पथिमथोः सर्वनामस्थाने ।

6.4.8 सर्वनामस्थाने चासम्बुद्धौ । penultimate vowel of stem ending in नकार is lengthened, except for Vocative, for सर्वनामस्थानम् affixes.

7.1.70 उगिदचां सर्वनामस्थाने अ-धातोः । non-dhatu stems that have उक् vowel as Tag letter get नुम् augment.

7.1.72 नपुंसकस्य झलचः । neuter stem ending in अच् or झल् gets नुम् augment when facing Sarvanamasthana affix.

7.1.86 इतोऽत् सर्वनामस्थाने ।

7.3.110 ऋतो ङिसर्वनामस्थानयोः ।

सर्व mfn - All, Everyone, Several (mfn, adjective usage)

सर्व	स् अ र् व् अ = stem अ ending, अकारान्तः masculine adjective			सुप् Affixes by 4.1.2, Tags by 1.3.2 to 1.3.9		
	1	2	3	1	2	3
V हे	सर्व 6.1.69	सर्वौ	सर्वे	similar to 1		
1	सर्वः 8.2.66 8.3.15	सर्वौ 6.1.88	सर्वे 7.1.17 6.1.87	स्	औ	ज् अस् → श् ई
2	सर्वम् 6.1.107	सर्वौ 6.1.88	सर्वान् 6.1.102 6.1.103	अम्	औ	अस्
3	सर्वेण 7.1.12 6.1.87 8.4.2	सर्वाभ्याम् 7.3.102	सर्वैः 7.1.9 6.1.88 8.2.66 8.3.15	ट् आ	भ्याम्	भिस् → ऐस्
4	सर्वस्मै 7.1.14	सर्वाभ्याम् 7.3.102	सर्वेभ्यः 7.3.103 8.2.66 8.3.15	(ङ्) ए → स्मै	भ्याम्	भ्यस्
5	सर्वस्मात् 7.1.15 6.1.101	सर्वाभ्याम् 7.3.102	सर्वेभ्यः 7.3.103 8.2.66 8.3.15	ङ् अस् ङँ	भ्याम्	भ्यस्
6	सर्वस्य 7.1.12	सर्वयोः 7.3.104 6.1.78 8.2.66 8.3.15	सर्वेषाम् 7.1.52 7.3.103 8.3.59	(ङ्) अस्	ओस्	आम् → स् उँ ट् + आम्
7	सर्वस्मिन् 7.1.15	सर्वयोः 7.3.104 6.1.78 8.2.66 8.3.15	सर्वेषु 7.3.103 8.3.59	(ङ्) इ →स्मिन्	ओस्	सु
विश्व sum total, अन्य another अन्यतर the second, इतर the rest/remaining out of two, एकतर one-sided, एकतम one-of-many, त्व-नेम-सम-सिम one other/several (these stems are synonyms), एक a/the						
Stems ending in डतर / डतम affixes - कतर कतम यतर यतम ततर ततम						

सर्वा feminine - All, Everyone

सर्वा	स् अ र् व् आ = stem आ ending, आकारान्तः feminine adjective			सुप् Affixes by 4.1.2, Tags by 1.3.2 to 1.3.9		
	1	2	3	1	2	3
V हे	सर्वे	सर्वे	सर्वाः	similar to 1		
1	सर्वे 8.2.66 8.3.15	सर्वे	सर्वाः 7.1.17 6.1.87	स्	औ	ज् अस् → श् ई
2	सर्वाम् 6.1.107	सर्वे	सर्वाः 6.1.102 6.1.103	अम्	औ	अस्
3	सर्वया 7.1.12 6.1.87 8.4.2	सर्वाभ्याम् 7.3.102	सर्वाभिः 7.1.9 6.1.88 8.2.66 8.3.15	ट् आ	भ्याम्	भिस् → ऐस्
4	सर्वस्यै 7.1.14	सर्वाभ्याम् 7.3.102	सर्वाभ्यः 7.3.103 8.2.66 8.3.15	(ङ्) ए → स्मै	भ्याम्	भ्यस्
5	सर्वस्याः 7.1.15 6.1.101	सर्वाभ्याम् 7.3.102	सर्वाभ्यः 7.3.103 8.2.66 8.3.15	ङ् अस् इँ	भ्याम्	भ्यस्
6	सर्वस्याः 7.1.12	सर्वयोः 7.3.104 6.1.78 8.2.66 8.3.15	सर्वासाम् 7.3.103	(ङ्) अस्	ओस्	आम् → स् उँ ट् + आम्
7	सर्वस्याम् 7.1.15	सर्वयोः 7.3.104 6.1.78 8.2.66 8.3.15	सर्वासु 7.3.103	(ङ्) इ →स्मिन्	ओस्	सु
विश्वा अन्या अन्यतरा इतरा त्वा नेमा समा एकतरा एकतमा, stems ending in डतर / डतम affixes get आ ending in feminine कतरा कतमा, यतरा यतमा, ततरा ततमा						

सर्व neuter - All, Everyone

सर्व	स् अ र् व् अ = अ ending neuter			सुप् Affixes by 4.1.2		
	1	2	3	1	2	3
V हे	सर्व	सर्वे	सर्वाणि	similar to 1		
1	सर्वम्	सर्वे	सर्वाणि	स्	औ	ज् अस् → श् ई
2	सर्वम्	सर्वे	सर्वाणि	अम्	औ	अस्
3	सर्वेण 7.1.12 6.1.87 8.4.2	सर्वाभ्याम् 7.3.102	सर्वैः 7.1.9 6.1.88 8.2.66 8.3.15	ट् आ	भ्याम्	भिस् → ऐस्
4	सर्वस्मै 7.1.14	सर्वाभ्याम् 7.3.102	सर्वेभ्यः 7.3.103 8.2.66 8.3.15	(ङ्) ए → स्मै	भ्याम्	भ्यस्
5	सर्वस्मात् 7.1.15 6.1.101	सर्वाभ्याम् 7.3.102	सर्वेभ्यः 7.3.103 8.2.66 8.3.15	ङ् अस् ईं	भ्याम्	भ्यस्
6	सर्वस्य 7.1.12	सर्वयोः 7.3.104 6.1.78 8.2.66 8.3.15	सर्वेषाम् 7.1.52 7.3.103 8.3.59	(ङ्) अस्	ओस्	आम् → स् उँ ट् + आम्
7	सर्वस्मिन् 7.1.15	सर्वयोः 7.3.104 6.1.78 8.2.66 8.3.15	सर्वेषु 7.3.103 8.3.59	(ङ्) इ →स्मिन्	ओस्	सु
Same as Stem सर्व Masculine from 3rd case onwards						
Similar stems विश्व, सम, एकतर, stems ending in डतर affix कतर यतर ततर						
However these stems are त् ending in neuter - अन्यत् अन्यतरत् इतरत् त्वत् एकतमत् and stems ending in डतम affix कतमत् यतमत् ततमत्						

विश्व mfn – (declines as सर्व)

उभ mfn - both, the two, pair (only in Dual)

उभ	उ भ् अ = masc/neuter अ ending, उभा feminine आ ending			सुप् Affixes by 4.1.2, Tags by 1.3.2 to 1.3.9		
	masc 2	feminine 2	neuter 2		2	
V हे	उभौ	उभे	उभे	similar to 1		
1	उभौ 6.1.88	उभे 6.1.88	उभे 7.1.17 6.1.87		औ	
2	उभौ 6.1.88	उभे 6.1.88	उभे 6.1.102 6.1.103		औ	
3	उभाभ्याम् 7.3.102	उभाभ्याम् 7.3.102	उभाभ्याम् 7.3.102		भ्याम्	
4	उभाभ्याम् 7.3.102	उभाभ्याम् 7.3.102	उभाभ्याम् 7.3.102		भ्याम्	
5	उभाभ्याम् 7.3.102	उभाभ्याम् 7.3.102	उभाभ्याम् 7.3.102		भ्याम्	
6	उभयोः 7.3.104 6.1.78 8.2.66 8.3.15	उभयोः 7.3.104 6.1.78 8.2.66 8.3.15	उभयोः 7.3.104 6.1.78 8.2.66 8.3.15		ओस्	
7	उभयोः 7.3.104 6.1.78 8.2.66 8.3.15	उभयोः 7.3.104 6.1.78 8.2.66 8.3.15	उभयोः 7.3.104 6.1.78 8.2.66 8.3.15		ओस्	
उभ declines only in dual number. There is no singular/plural						

उभय mfn - to both sides, in two ways (has no Dual)

उभय	उ भ् अ य् अ = adjective stem अ ending, अकारान्तः masculine			सुप् Affixes by 4.1.2, Tags by 1.3.2 to 1.3.9		
	1		3	1		3
V हे	उभय 6.1.69		उभये	similar to 1		
1	उभयः 8.2.66 8.3.15		उभये 7.1.17 6.1.87	स्		ज् अस् → श् ई
2	उभयम् 6.1.107		उभयान् 6.1.102 6.1.103	अम्		अस्
3	उभयेन 7.1.12 6.1.87		उभयैः 7.1.9 6.1.88 8.2.66 8.3.15	ट् आ		भिस् → ऐस्
4	उभयस्मै 7.1.14		उभयेभ्यः 7.3.103 8.2.66 8.3.15	(ङ्) ए → स्मै		भ्यस्
5	उभयस्मात् 7.1.15 6.1.101		उभयेभ्यः 7.3.103 8.2.66 8.3.15	ङ् अस् इँ		भ्यस्
6	उभयस्य 7.1.12		उभयेषाम् 7.1.52 7.3.103 8.3.59	(ङ्) अस्		आम् → स् उँ ट् + आम्
7	उभयस्मिन् 7.1.15		उभयेषु 7.3.103 8.3.59	(ङ्) इ → स्मिन्		सु

उभय declines in singular and plural number. There is no dual. It is constructed from उभ + तयप् (अयच्) Taddhita Affix

उभयी feminine (has no Dual)

उभयी	उ भ् अ य् ई = adjective stem ई ending, ईकारान्तः feminine			सुप् Affixes by 4.1.2, Tags by 1.3.2 to 1.3.9		
	1		3	1		3
V हे	उभयि 6.1.69		उभय्यः	similar to 1		
1	उभयी 8.2.66 8.3.15		उभय्यः 7.1.17 6.1.87	स्		ज् अस् → श् ई
2	उभयीम् 6.1.107		उभयीः 6.1.102 6.1.103	अम्		अस्
3	उभय्या 7.1.12 6.1.87		उभयीभिः 7.1.9 6.1.88 8.2.66 8.3.15	ट् आ		भिस् → ऐस्
4	उभय्यै 7.1.14		उभयीभ्यः 7.3.103 8.2.66 8.3.15	(ङ्) ए → स्मै		भ्यस्
5	उभय्याः 7.1.15 6.1.101		उभयीभ्यः 7.3.103 8.2.66 8.3.15	ङ् अस् इँ		भ्यस्
6	उभय्याः 7.1.12		उभयीनाम् 7.3.103	(ङ्) अस्		आम् → स् उँ ट् + आम्
7	उभय्याम् 7.1.15		उभयीषु 7.3.103 8.3.59	(ङ्) इ → स्मिन्		सु
उभयी declines in singular and plural number. There is no dual. Constructed from उभ + तयप् (अयच्) Taddhita Affix + ई feminine. Declines similar to नदी						

उभय neuter (has no Dual)

उभय	उ भ् अ य् अ = adjective stem अ ending, अकारान्तः neuter			सुप् Affixes by 4.1.2, Tags by 1.3.2 to 1.3.9		
	1		3	1		3
V हे	उभय 6.1.69		उभयानि	similar to 1		
1	उभयम् 8.2.66 8.3.15		उभयानि 7.1.17 6.1.87	स्		ज् अस् → श् ई
2	उभयम् 6.1.107		उभयानि 6.1.102 6.1.103	अम्		अस्
3	उभयेण 7.1.12 6.1.87		उभयैः 7.1.9 6.1.88 8.2.66 8.3.15	ट् आ		भिस् → ऐस्
4	उभयाय 7.1.14		उभयेभ्यः 7.3.103 8.2.66 8.3.15	(ङ्) ए → स्मै		भ्यस्
5	उभयात् 7.1.15 6.1.101		उभयेभ्यः 7.3.103 8.2.66 8.3.15	ङ् अस् इँ		भ्यस्
6	उभयस्य 7.1.12		उभयाणाम् 7.3.103 8.3.59	(ङ्) अस्		आम् → स् उँ ट् + आम्
7	उभये 7.1.15		उभयेषु 7.3.103 8.3.59	(ङ्) इ → स्मिन्		सु

उभय declines in singular and plural number. There is no dual.
It is constructed from उभ + तयप् (अयच्) Taddhita Affix.
Declines similar to फल neuter.

डतर mf – (कतर यतर ततर decline as सर्व)

कतर n – who or what out of two (interrogative usage)

कतर	क् अ त् अ र् अ = अ ending neuter interrogative			सुप् Affixes by 4.1.2, Tags by 1.3.2 to 1.3.9		
	1	2	3	1	2	3
1	कतरत् 8.2.66 8.3.15	कतरे 6.1.88	कतराणि 7.1.17 6.1.87	स्	औ	ज् अस् → श् ई
2	कतरत् 6.1.107	कतरे 6.1.88	कतराणि 6.1.102 6.1.103	अम्	औ	अस्
3	कतरेण 7.1.12 6.1.87 8.4.2	कतराभ्याम् 7.3.102	कतरैः 7.1.9 6.1.88 8.2.66 8.3.15	ट् आ	भ्याम्	भिस् → ऐस्
4	कतरस्मै 7.1.14	कतराभ्याम् 7.3.102	कतरेभ्यः 7.3.103 8.2.66 8.3.15	(ङ्) ए → स्मै	भ्याम्	भ्यस्
5	कतरस्मात् 7.1.15 6.1.101	कतराभ्याम् 7.3.102	कतरेभ्यः 7.3.103 8.2.66 8.3.15	ङ् अस् ङँ	भ्याम्	भ्यस्
6	कतरस्य 7.1.12	कतरयोः 7.3.104 6.1.78 8.2.66 8.3.15	कतरेषाम् 7.1.52 7.3.103 8.3.59	(ङ्) अस्	ओस्	आम् → स् उँ ट् + आम्
7	कतरस्मिन् 7.1.15	कतरयोः 7.3.104 6.1.78 8.2.66 8.3.15	कतरेषु 7.3.103 8.3.59	(ङ्) इ →स्मिन्	ओस्	सु
Interrogative pronouns do not have Vocative. Declines as सर्व। Becomes तकारान्त in 1/1 and 2/1						

डतम mf – (कतम यतम ततम decline as सर्व)

कतम n – who or what out of many (interrogative)

कतम	क् अ त् अ म् अ = अ ending neuter interrogative			सुप् Affixes by 4.1.2, Tags by 1.3.2 to 1.3.9		
	1	2	3	1	2	3
1	कतमत् 8.2.66 8.3.15	कतमे 6.1.88	कतमानि 7.1.17 6.1.87	स्	औ	ज् अस् → श् ई
2	कतमत् 6.1.107	कतमे 6.1.88	कतमानि 6.1.102 6.1.103	अम्	औ	अस्
3	कतमेन 7.1.12 6.1.87 8.4.2	कतमाभ्याम् 7.3.102	कतमैः 7.1.9 6.1.88 8.2.66 8.3.15	ट् आ	भ्याम्	भिस् → ऐस्
4	कतमस्मै 7.1.14	कतमाभ्याम् 7.3.102	कतमेभ्यः 7.3.103 8.2.66 8.3.15	(ङ्) ए → स्मै	भ्याम्	भ्यस्
5	कतमस्मात् 7.1.15 6.1.101	कतमाभ्याम् 7.3.102	कतमेभ्यः 7.3.103 8.2.66 8.3.15	ङ् अस् इँ	भ्याम्	भ्यस्
6	कतमस्य 7.1.12	कतमयोः 7.3.104 6.1.78 8.2.66 8.3.15	कतमेषाम् 7.1.52 7.3.103 8.3.59	(ङ्) अस्	ओस्	आम् → स् उँ ट् + आम्
7	कतमस्मिन् 7.1.15	कतमयोः 7.3.104 6.1.78 8.2.66 8.3.15	कतमेषु 7.3.103 8.3.59	(ङ्) इ →स्मिन्	ओस्	सु
Interrogative pronouns do not have Vocative. Declines as सर्व । Becomes तकारान्त in 1/1 and 2/1						

अन्य mf – (declines as सर्व)

अन्य n – (declines as सर्व 3rd case onwards)

अन्यतर mf – (declines as सर्व)

अन्यतर n – (declines as सर्व 3rd case onwards)

इतर mf – (declines as सर्व)

इतर n – (declines as सर्व 3rd case onwards)

त्वत् mf – Other, other one, other thing

त्वत्	तकारान्तः	Masc/feminine		सुप् Affixes		
	1	2	3	1	2	3
1	त्वत् 6.1.68 8.2.39 8.4.56	त्वतौ	त्वतः 8.2.66 8.3.15	स्	औ	अस्
2	त्वतम्	त्वतौ	त्वतः 8.2.66 8.3.15	अम्	औ	अस्
3	त्वता	त्वद्भ्याम् 8.2.39	त्वद्भिः 8.2.39 8.2.66 8.3.15	आ	भ्याम्	भिस्
4	त्वते	त्वद्भ्याम् 8.2.39	त्वद्भ्यः 8.2.39 8.2.66 8.3.15	ए	भ्याम्	भ्यस्
5	त्वतः 8.2.66 8.3.15	त्वद्भ्याम् 8.2.39	त्वद्भ्यः 8.2.39 8.2.66 8.3.15	अस्	भ्याम्	भ्यस्
6	त्वतः 8.2.66 8.3.15	त्वतोः 8.2.66 8.3.15	त्वताम्	अस्	ओस्	आम्
7	त्वति	त्वतोः 8.2.66 8.3.15	त्वत्सु 8.2.39 8.4.55	इ	ओस्	सु
Declines similar to मरुत् m. There is no Vocative						

त्वत् n – Other, other thing

त्वत्	तकारान्तः	त्	f	सुप् Affixes		
	1	2	3			
1	त्वत् 6.1.68 8.2.39 8.4.56	त्वतौ	त्वतः 8.2.66 8.3.15	स्	औ	अस्
2	त्वतम्	त्वतौ	त्वतः 8.2.66 8.3.15	अम्	औ	अस्
3	त्वता	त्वद्भ्याम् 8.2.39	त्वद्भिः 8.2.39 8.2.66 8.3.15	आ	भ्याम्	भिस्
4	त्वते	त्वद्भ्याम् 8.2.39	त्वद्भ्यः 8.2.39 8.2.66 8.3.15	ए	भ्याम्	भ्यस्
5	त्वतः 8.2.66 8.3.15	त्वद्भ्याम् 8.2.39	त्वद्भ्यः 8.2.39 8.2.66 8.3.15	अस्	भ्याम्	भ्यस्
6	त्वतः 8.2.66 8.3.15	त्वतोः 8.2.66 8.3.15	त्वताम्	अस्	ओस्	आम्
7	त्वति	त्वतोः 8.2.66 8.3.15	त्वत्सु 8.2.39 8.4.55	इ	ओस्	सु
Declines similar to जगत् n. There is no Vocative						

त्वत्	तकारान्तः	त्	m	त्वत्	त्	n
1	त्वत्	त्वतौ	त्वतः	त्वत्	त्वती	त्वन्ति
2	त्वतम्	त्वतौ	त्वतः	त्वत्	त्वती	त्वन्ति
3	त्वता	त्वद्भ्याम्	त्वद्भिः	त्वता	त्वद्भ्याम्	त्वद्भिः
4	त्वते	त्वद्भ्याम्	त्वद्भ्यः	त्वते	त्वद्भ्याम्	त्वद्भ्यः
5	त्वतः	त्वद्भ्याम्	त्वद्भ्यः	त्वतः	त्वद्भ्याम्	त्वद्भ्यः
6	त्वतः	त्वतोः	त्वताम्	त्वतः	त्वतोः	त्वताम्
7	त्वति	त्वतोः	त्वत्सु	त्वति	त्वतोः	त्वत्सु
V	हे त्वत्	हे त्वतौ	हे त्वतः	हे त्वत्	हे त्वती	हे त्वन्ति
	Other			Other		
Template मरुत् m (2nd case onwards)				Template जगत् n		

त्वत्	तकारान्तः	त्	f
1	त्वत्	त्वतौ	त्वतः
2	त्वतम्	त्वतौ	त्वतः
3	त्वता	त्वद्भ्याम्	त्वद्भिः
4	त्वते	त्वद्भ्याम्	त्वद्भ्यः
5	त्वतः	त्वद्भ्याम्	त्वद्भ्यः
6	त्वतः	त्वतोः	त्वताम्
7	त्वति	त्वतोः	त्वत्सु
V	हे त्वत्	हे त्वतौ	हे त्वतः
	Other		
	Template सरित् f , Identical to त्वत् m		

त्व mfn – (declines as सर्व)

नेम mn - One half, a portion

नेम	न् ए म् अ = masc/neuter stem अ ending, अकारान्तः			सुप् Affixes by 4.1.2, Tags by 1.3.2 to 1.3.9		
	1	2	3	1	2	3
1	नेमः 8.2.66 8.3.15	नेमौ 6.1.88	नेमाः / नेमे 8.2.66 8.3.15 / 1.1.33	स्	औ	अस्
2	नेमम् 6.1.107	नेमौ 6.1.88	नेमान् 6.1.102 6.1.103	अम्	औ	अस्
3	नेमेन 7.1.12 6.1.87	नेमाभ्याम् 7.3.102	नेमैः 7.1.9 8.2.66 6.1.88 8.3.15	आ	भ्याम्	भिस्
4	नेमाय 7.1.13 7.3.102	नेमाभ्याम् 7.3.102	नेमेभ्यः 7.3.103 8.2.66 8.3.15	(ङ्) ए	भ्याम्	भ्यस्
5	नेमात् 7.1.12 6.1.101	नेमाभ्याम् 7.3.102	रामेभ्यः 7.3.103 8.2.66 8.3.15	ङ् अस् इँ	भ्याम्	भ्यस्
6	नेमस्य 7.1.12	नेमयोः 7.3.104 6.1.78 8.2.66 8.3.15	नेमानाम् 7.1.54 6.4.3	(ङ्) अस्	ओस्	आम्
7	नेमे 6.1.87	नेमयोः 7.3.104 6.1.78 8.2.66 8.3.15	नेमेषु 7.3.103 8.3.59	(ङ्) इ	ओस्	सु
There is no Vocative. Similar stems प्रथम the first चरम last अल्प small अर्ध half कतिपय few द्वय two त्रय three.						

नेमा f - One half, a portion

सम mfn – one other portion (declines as सर्व)

सिम mfn – another part (declines as सर्व)

पूर्व Prior, Eastern (mfn, adjective usage, पूर्वा f , पूर्व n)

पूर्व	प् उ र् व् अ = stem अ ending, अकारान्तः masculine adjective			सुप् Affixes by 4.1.2, Tags by 1.3.2 to 1.3.9		
	1	2	3	1	2	3
V हे	पूर्व 6.1.69	पूर्वौ	पूर्वे / पूर्वाः	similar to 1		
1	पूर्वः 8.2.66 8.3.15	पूर्वौ 6.1.88	पूर्वे / पूर्वाः 7.1.17 6.1.87 / 7.1.16	स्	औ	ज् अस् → श् ई
2	पूर्वम् 6.1.107	पूर्वौ 6.1.88	पूर्वान् 6.1.102 6.1.103	अम्	औ	अस्
3	पूर्वेण 7.1.12 6.1.87 8.4.2	पूर्वाभ्याम् 7.3.102	पूर्वैः 7.1.9 6.1.88 8.2.66 8.3.15	ट् आ	भ्याम्	भिस् → ऐस्
4	पूर्वस्मै 7.1.14	पूर्वाभ्याम् 7.3.102	पूर्वेभ्यः 7.3.103 8.2.66 8.3.15	(ङ्) ए → स्मै	भ्याम्	भ्यस्
5	पूर्वस्मात् / पूर्वात् 7.1.15 6.1.101 / 7.1.16	पूर्वाभ्याम् 7.3.102	पूर्वेभ्यः 7.3.103 8.2.66 8.3.15	ङ् अस् ङँ	भ्याम्	भ्यस्
6	पूर्वस्य 7.1.12	पूर्वयोः 7.3.104 6.1.78 8.2.66 8.3.15	पूर्वेषाम् 7.1.52 7.3.103 8.3.59	(ङ्) अस्	ओस्	आम् → स् उँ ट् + आम्
7	पूर्वस्मिन् / पूर्वे 7.1.15 / 7.1.16	पूर्वयोः 7.3.104 6.1.78 8.2.66 8.3.15	पूर्वेषु 7.3.103 8.3.59	(ङ्) इ → स्मिन्	ओस्	सु
Similar Stems पर later, subsequent, transcendental, beyond the						

senses, highest. अवर inferior दक्षिण southern, to the right उत्तर northern, to the left अपर lesser, not the highest अधर lower स्व oneself अन्तर something external that is closest

पर अवर दक्षिण उत्तर अपर अध (decline as पूर्व)

स्व One's own, oneself, personal possesion

स्व	अकारान्तः	अ	mfn
1	स्वः	स्वौ	स्वाः
2	स्वम्	स्वौ	स्वान्
3	स्वेन	स्वाभ्याम्	स्वैः
4	स्वाय	स्वाभ्याम्	स्वेभ्यः
5	स्वात्	स्वाभ्याम्	स्वेभ्यः
6	स्वस्य	स्वयोः	स्वानाम्
7	स्वे	स्वयोः	स्वेषु
personal pronoun			
Template राम m			

अन्तर (declines as पूर्व)

त्यद् (declines as तद्)

तद् एतद् m

तद्	दकारान्तः	द्	m	एतद्	द्	m
1	सः	तौ	ते	एषः	एतौ	एते
2	तम्	तौ	तान्	एतम् , एनम्	एतौ , एनौ	एतान् , एनान्
3	तेन	ताभ्याम्	तैः	एतेन , एनेन	एताभ्याम्	एतैः
4	तस्मै	ताभ्याम्	तेभ्यः	एतस्मै	एताभ्याम्	एतेभ्यः
5	तस्मात्	ताभ्याम्	तेभ्यः	एतस्मात्	एताभ्याम्	एतेभ्यः
6	तस्य	तयोः	तेषाम्	एतस्य	एतयोः , एनयोः	एतेषाम्
7	तस्मिन्	तयोः	तेषु	एतस्मिन्	एतयोः , एनयोः	एतेषु
	He, his, that male, theirs			He, his, this male, theirs		
	त्यद् that, indeed					

The optional forms एनम् , एनेन , etc. are to be used when there is an अन्वादेश , i.e. the main form has already been used once, and the paragraph is further continuing.

तद् एतद् f

तद्	दकारान्तः	द्	f	एतद्	द्	f
1	सा	ते	ताः	एषा	एते	एताः
2	ताम्	ते	ताः	एताम् , एनाम्	एते , एने	एताः , एनाः
3	तया	ताभ्याम्	ताभिः	एतया , एनया	एताभ्याम्	एताभिः
4	तस्यै	ताभ्याम्	ताभ्यः	एतस्यै	एताभ्याम्	एताभ्यः
5	तस्याः	ताभ्याम्	ताभ्यः	एतस्याः	एताभ्याम्	एताभ्यः
6	तस्याः	तयोः	तासाम्	एतस्याः	एतयोः , एनयोः	एतासाम्
7	तस्याम्	तयोः	तासु	एतस्याम्	एतयोः , एनयोः	एतासु
sHe, her, that female, theirs				sHe, her, this female, theirs		
त्यद् f that, indeed						

Note - Use the optional form at the time of subsequent mention of a thing already mentioned, not in first use.

तद् एतद् n

तद्	दकारान्तः	द्	n	तद्	द्	n
1	तत्	ते	तानि	एतत्	एते	एतानि
2	तत्	ते	तानि	एतत्	एते	एतानि
3	तेन	ताभ्याम्	तैः	एतेन	एताभ्याम्	एतैः
4	तस्मै	ताभ्याम्	तेभ्यः	एतस्मै	एताभ्याम्	एतेभ्यः
5	तस्मात्	ताभ्याम्	तेभ्यः	एतस्मात्	एताभ्याम्	एतेभ्यः
6	तस्य	तयोः	तेषाम्	एतस्य	एतयोः , एनयोः	एतेषाम्
7	तस्मिन्	तयोः	तेषु	एतस्मिन्	एतयोः , एनयोः	एतेषु
it, that, that neuter, it's, theirs				It, this, this neuter, it's, theirs		
Template तद् m (3rd case onwards)				Template एतद् m (3rd case onwards)		
त्यद् n that, indeed						

यद् mn

यद्	दकारान्तः	द्	m	यद्	द्	neuter
1	यः	यौ	ये	यत्	ये	यानि
2	यम्	यौ	यान्	यत्	ये	यानि
3	येन	याभ्याम्	यैः	येन	याभ्याम्	यैः
4	यस्मै	याभ्याम्	येभ्यः	यस्मै	याभ्याम्	येभ्यः
5	यस्मात्	याभ्याम्	येभ्यः	यस्मात्	याभ्याम्	येभ्यः
6	यस्य	ययोः	येषाम्	यस्य	ययोः	येषाम्
7	यस्मिन्	ययोः	येषु	यस्मिन्	ययोः	येषु
Who, the one that (male)				Who, it, that (neuter)		
यतरद् mn , यतमद् mn				Template यद् m (3rd case onwards)		

यद् f - Who, the one that

यद्	दकारान्तः	द्	feminine
1	या	ये	याः
2	याम्	ये	याः
3	यया	याभ्याम्	याभिः
4	यस्यै	याभ्याम्	याभ्यः
5	यस्याः	याभ्याम्	याभ्यः
6	यस्याः	ययोः	यासाम्
7	यस्याम्	ययोः	यासु
यतरद् , यतमद् in that of the two			

इदम् mn

इदम् मकारान्तः म्			m	इदम्	म्	n
1	अयम्	इमौ	इमे	इदम्	इमे	इमानि
2	इमम्, एनम्	इमौ,एनौ	इमान्, एनान्	इदम्, एनत्	इमे,एने	इमानि, एनानि
3	अनेन, एनेन	आभ्याम्	एभिः	अनेन, एनेन	आभ्याम्	एभिः
4	अस्मै	आभ्याम्	एभ्यः	अस्मै	आभ्याम्	एभ्यः
5	अस्मात्	आभ्याम्	एभ्यः	अस्मात्	आभ्याम्	एभ्यः
6	अस्य	अनयोः,एनयोः	एषाम्	अस्य	अनयोः,एनयोः	एषाम्
7	अस्मिन्	अनयोः,एनयोः	एषु	अस्मिन्	अनयोः,एनयोः	एषु
This (closest e.g. अक्ष soul). Usage in Upanishads				This (closest e.g. शरीरम् body). Usage in Upanishads		
				Template इदम् m (3rd case onwards)		

1/1 अयम् this, 2/1 इमम् this, 3/1 अनेन by this, 4/1 अस्मै to this, 5/1 अस्मात् from this, 6/1 अस्य of this, 7/1 अस्मिन् in this

इदम् f

इदम्	मकारान्तः	म्	f
1	इयम्	इमे	इमाः
2	इमाम्, एनाम्	इमे,एने	इमाः, एनाः
3	अनया, एनया	आभ्याम्	आभिः
4	अस्यै	आभ्याम्	आभ्यः
5	अस्याः	आभ्याम्	आभ्यः
6	अस्याः	अनयोः,एनयोः	आसाम्
7	अस्याम्	अनयोः,एनयोः	आसु
This (closest e.g. मति intellect) Usage in Upanishads			

अदस् mn

अदस्	सकारान्तः	स्	m	अदस्	स्	n
1	असौ	अमू	अमी	अदः	अमू	अमूनि
2	अमुम्	अमू	अमून्	अदः	अमू	अमूनि
3	अमुना	अमूभ्यां	अमीभिः	अमुना	अमूभ्यां	अमीभिः
4	अमुष्मै	अमूभ्यां	अमीभ्यः	अमुष्मै	अमूभ्यां	अमीभ्यः
5	अमुष्मात्	अमूभ्यां	अमीभ्यः	अमुष्मात्	अमूभ्यां	अमीभ्यः
6	अमुष्य	अमुयोः	अमषाम्	अमुष्य	अमुयोः	अमषाम्
7	अमुष्मिन्	अमुयोः	अमीषु	अमुष्मिन्	अमुयोः	अमीषु
This (over there, e.g. वृक्षः tree), Usage in Upanishads				This (over there, e.g. गृहम् house), Usage in Upanishads, Template अदस् m (3rd case onwards)		

अदस् f

अदस्	सकारान्तः	स्	f
1	असौ	अमू	अमूः
2	अमूम्	अमू	अमूः
3	अमुया	अमूभ्यां	अमूभिः
4	अमुष्यै	अमूभ्यां	अमूभ्यः
5	अमुष्याः	अमूभ्यां	अमूभ्यः
6	अमुष्याः	अमुयोः	अमूषाम्
7	अमुष्याम्	अमुयोः	अमूषु
This (over there, e.g. लता creeper), Usage in Upanishads			

एक a, the (declines as सर्व)

However if these words are not used to mean numeral one, but the article “a”, then they will decline in a 7x3 matrix, with template सर्व ।

एक		अ	m	एका	आ	f	एक	अ	n
1	एकः	एकौ	एके	एका	एके	एकाः	एकम्	एके	एकानि
2	एकम्	एकौ	एकान्	एकाम्	एके	एकाः	एकम्	एके	एकानि
3	एकेन	एकाभ्यां	एकैः	एकया	एकाभ्यां	एका भिः	सर्वेण	एकाभ्यां	एकैः
4	एकस्मै	एकाभ्यां	एकेभ्यः	एकस्यै	ऐकाभ्यां	एका भ्यः	एकस्मै	एकाभ्यां	एकेभ्यः
5	एकस्मात्	एकाभ्यां	एकेभ्यः	एकस्याः	ऐकाभ्यां	एका भ्यः	एकस्मात्	एकाभ्यां	एकेभ्यः
6	एकस्य	एकयोः	एकेषां	एकस्याः	एकयोः	एकासाम्	एकस्य	एकयोः	एकेषां
7	एकस्मिन्	एकयोः	एकेषु	एकस्यां	एकयोः	एकासु	एकस्मिन्	एकयोः	एकेषु
V हे	एक	एकौ	एके	एके	एके	एकाः	एक	एके	एकानि

Article “a”, “the”

Usage not in the sense of number but as Article Adjective.

(For numeral usage it has only singular case, and there is no vocative).

द्वि mfn – the two, pair, both (only in Dual)

द्वि	द् व् इ = stem इ ending			सुप् Affixes by 4.1.2, Tags by 1.3.2 to 1.3.9	
	2 masc	2 feminine	2 neuter		2
1	द्वौ	द्वे 6.1.88	द्वे		औ
2	द्वौ	द्वे 6.1.88	द्वे		औ
3	द्वाभ्याम्	द्वाभ्याम् 7.3.102	द्वाभ्याम्		भ्याम्
4	द्वाभ्याम्	द्वाभ्याम् 7.3.102	द्वाभ्याम्		भ्याम्
5	द्वाभ्याम्	द्वाभ्याम् 7.3.102	द्वाभ्याम्		भ्याम्
6	द्वयोः	द्वयोः	द्वयोः		ओस्
7	द्वयोः	द्वयोः	द्वयोः		ओस्
Masculine and Neuter decline as अकारान्त द्व (राम) stem. Feminine declines as आकारान्त द्वा (रमा) stem. (called इकारान्त due to ganapatha entry द्वि). There is no Vocative, as it is used in the sense of numeral only.					

युष्मद् mfn – YOU (personal pronoun)

युष्मद्	य् उ ष् म् अ द् = द् ending दकारान्तः identical in masc/feminine/neuter			सुप् Affixes by 4.1.2, Tags by 1.3.2 to 1.3.9		
	1	2	3	1	2	3
1	त्वम् 8.2.66 8.3.15	युवाम् 6.1.88	यूयम् 7.1.17 6.1.87	स्	औ	ज् अस् → श् ई
2	त्वाम् / त्वा 6.1.107	कतमे 6.1.88	कतमानि 6.1.102 6.1.103	अम्	औ	अस्
3	त्वया 7.1.12 6.1.87 8.4.2	कतमाभ्याम् 7.3.102	कतमैः 7.1.9 6.1.88 8.2.66 8.3.15	ट् आ	भ्याम्	भिस् → ऐस्
4	तुभ्यम् / ते 7.1.14	कतमाभ्याम् 7.3.102	कतमेभ्यः 7.3.103 8.2.66 8.3.15	(ङ्) ए → स्मै	भ्याम्	भ्यस्
5	त्वत् 7.1.15 6.1.101	कतमाभ्याम् 7.3.102	कतमेभ्यः 7.3.103 8.2.66 8.3.15	ङ् अस् इँ	भ्याम्	भ्यस्
6	तव / ते 7.1.12	कतमयोः 7.3.104 6.1.78 8.2.66 8.3.15	कतमेषाम् 7.1.52 7.3.103 8.3.59	(ङ्) अस्	ओस्	आम् → स् उँ ट् + आम्
7	त्वयि 7.1.15	कतमयोः 7.3.104 6.1.78 8.2.66 8.3.15	कतमेषु 7.3.103 8.3.59	(ङ्) इ → स्मिन्	ओस्	सु
Personal pronouns do not have Vocative.						
thou, you, your, yours. In texts, वः is seen as वो by visarga sandhi. वाम् is seen as वां by anusvara sandhi.						

i.e.

for the sentence 'and mine' we will only use मम च and not मे च।

for the sentence 'and to me' we will only use मह्यम च and not मे च।

अस्मद् mfn – I (personal pronoun)

अस्मद्	दकारान्तः	द्	mfn
1	अहम्	आवाम्	वयम्
2	माम् , मा	आवाम् , नौ	अस्मान् , नः
3	मया	आवाभ्याम्	अस्माभिः
4	मह्यम् , मे	आवाभ्याम् , नौ	अस्मभ्यम् , नः
5	मत्	आवाभ्याम्	अस्मत्
6	मम , मे	आवयोः , नौ	अस्माकम् , नः
7	मयि	आवयोः	अस्मासु
I, we, me, my, mine, our			
In vedic texts, नः is seen as नो by visarga sandhi			
Personal pronouns do not have Vocative.			

The optional forms मा, मे, नौ, नः etc are not used while:

- Beginning a sentence
- Beginning a verse
- Beginning a पाद् of a श्लोक
- Before particles च, ह, हा, अह, एव

भवत् m - Thee, your honour, respectful address

भवत्	तकारान्तः	त्	m
1	भवान् 6.4.14 7.1.70 6.1.68 8.2.23	भवन्तौ 7.1.70 8.3.24 8.4.58	भवन्तः 7.1.70 8.3.24 8.4.58 8.2.66 8.3.15
2	भवन्तम् 7.1.70 8.3.24 8.4.58	भवन्तौ 7.1.70 8.3.24 8.4.58	भवतः
3	भवता	भवद्भ्याम्	भवद्भिः
4	भवते	भवद्भ्याम्	भवद्भ्यः
5	भवतः	भवद्भ्याम्	भवद्भ्यः
6	भवतः	भवतोः	भवताम्
7	भवति	भवतोः	भवत्सु
भवत् is actually listed in Ganapatha as भवतुँ = भवत् उँ, hence 7.1.70 applies			
Template धीमत् m, (2/3 case onwards same as मरुत्)			

Note while addressing a Guru or very senior person, we use the plural form instead of singular form. Otherwise for addressing someone respectfully (even a child or a friend) we use the singular form.

भवती f - Thee, your honour, respectful address

भवती	ईकारान्तः	ई	f
1	भवती	भवत्यौ	भवत्यः
2	भवतीम्	भवत्यौ	भवतीः
3	भवत्या	नदीभ्याम्	भवतीभिः
4	भवत्यै	नदीभ्याम्	भवतीभ्यः
5	भवत्याः	नदीभ्याम्	भवतीभ्यः
6	भवत्याः	भवत्योः	भवतीनाम्
7	भवत्याम्	भवत्योः	भवतीषु
Thee, your honour female, respectful address to a senior person			
Template नदी f			

Further to the respect aspect plural or singular usage, these words are used with the 3rd person प्रथम पुरुषः verb form as in Your honour goes –

भवान् गच्छति / भवती गच्छति । (correct)

भवान् गच्छसि / भवती गच्छसि (incorrect spelling)

So, in the verb usage, apply the 3rd person and not the 2nd person, even though the noun is a 2nd person word!

भवत् n – a revered thing, a photograph/statue

भवत्	तकारान्तः	त्	n
1	भवान्	भवती	भवन्ति
2	भवान्	भवती	भवन्ति
3	भवता	भवद्भ्याम्	भवद्भिः
4	भवते	भवद्भ्याम्	भवद्भ्यः
5	भवतः	भवद्भ्याम्	भवद्भ्यः
6	भवतः	भवतोः	भवताम्
7	भवति	भवतोः	भवत्सु
Thee, your honour, when spoken to the Divine or a reverential element or principle			
Template जगत् n			

किम् mfn - who, what (interrogative usage)

किम्	क् इ म् = stem म् ending, मकारान्तः masculine interrogative			सुप् Affixes by 4.1.2, Tags by 1.3.2 to 1.3.9		
	1	2	3	1	2	3
1	कः 8.2.66 8.3.15	कौ 6.1.88	के 7.1.17 6.1.87	स्	औ	ज् अस् → श् ई
2	कम् 6.1.107	कौ 6.1.88	कान् 6.1.102 6.1.103	अम्	औ	अस्
3	केन 7.1.12 6.1.87 8.4.2	काभ्याम् 7.3.102	कैः 7.1.9 6.1.88 8.2.66 8.3.15	ट् आ	भ्याम्	भिस् → ऐस्
4	कस्मै 7.1.14	काभ्याम् 7.3.102	केभ्यः 7.3.103 8.2.66 8.3.15	(ङ्) ए → स्मै	भ्याम्	भ्यस्
5	कस्मात् 7.1.15 6.1.101	काभ्याम् 7.3.102	केभ्यः 7.3.103 8.2.66 8.3.15	ङ् अस् ङँ	भ्याम्	भ्यस्
6	कस्य 7.1.12	कयोः 7.3.104 6.1.78 8.2.66 8.3.15	केषाम् 7.1.52 7.3.103 8.3.59	(ङ्) अस्	ओस्	आम् → स् उँ ट् + आम्
7	कस्मिन् 7.1.15	कयोः 7.3.104 6.1.78 8.2.66 8.3.15	केषु 7.3.103 8.3.59	(ङ्) इ →स्मिन्	ओस्	सु
Declines as क – अकारान्त, सर्व (called मकारान्त due to ganapatha entry किम्), Similar stems कतर कतम. Interrogative pronouns do not have Vocative. कतरम् , कतमम् which of the two? Template यद् m (3rd case onwards)						

Note कतरम् – कतरत् १/१ , कतरत् २/१कतमम् – कतमत् १/१, कतमत् २/१

किम् f - who, what (interrogative usage)

किम्	क् इ म् = stem म् ending, मकारान्तः feminine interrogative			सुप् Affixes by 4.1.2, Tags by 1.3.2 to 1.3.9		
	1	2	3	1	2	3
1	का 8.2.66 8.3.15	कौ 6.1.88	के 7.1.17 6.1.87	स्	औ	ज् अस् → श् ई
2	काम् 6.1.107	कौ 6.1.88	कान् 6.1.102 6.1.103	अम्	औ	अस्
3	कया 7.1.12 6.1.87 8.4.2	काभ्याम् 7.3.102	कैः 7.1.9 6.1.88 8.2.66 8.3.15	ट् आ	भ्याम्	भिस् → ऐस्
4	कस्यै 7.1.14	काभ्याम् 7.3.102	केभ्यः 7.3.103 8.2.66 8.3.15	(ङ्) ए → स्मै	भ्याम्	भ्यस्
5	कस्याः 7.1.15 6.1.101	काभ्याम् 7.3.102	केभ्यः 7.3.103 8.2.66 8.3.15	ङ् अस् इँ	भ्याम्	भ्यस्
6	कस्याः 7.1.12	कयोः 7.3.104 6.1.78 8.2.66 8.3.15	केषाम् 7.1.52 7.3.103 8.3.59	(ङ्) अस्	ओस्	आम् → स् उँ ट् + आम्
7	कस्याम् 7.1.15	कयोः 7.3.104 6.1.78 8.2.66 8.3.15	केषु 7.3.103 8.3.59	(ङ्) इ →स्मिन्	ओस्	सु
Declines as का – आकारान्त, सर्वा (called मकारान्त due to ganapatha entry किम्), Similar stems कतरा कतमा Interrogative pronouns do not have Vocative						

किम् neuter - who, what (interrogative usage)

किम्	क् इ म् = म् ending neuter interrogative			सुप् Affixes by 4.1.2, Tags by 1.3.2 to 1.3.9		
	1	2	3	1	2	3
1	किम् 8.2.66 8.3.15	के 6.1.88	कानि 7.1.17 6.1.87	स्	औ	ज् अस् → श् ई
2	किम् 6.1.107	के 6.1.88	कानि 6.1.102 6.1.103	अम्	औ	अस्
3	केन 7.1.12 6.1.87 8.4.2	काभ्याम् 7.3.102	कैः 7.1.9 6.1.88 8.2.66 8.3.15	ट् आ	भ्याम्	भिस् → ऐस्
4	कस्मै 7.1.14	काभ्याम् 7.3.102	केभ्यः 7.3.103 8.2.66 8.3.15	(ङ्) ए → स्मै	भ्याम्	भ्यस्
5	कस्मात् 7.1.15 6.1.101	काभ्याम् 7.3.102	केभ्यः 7.3.103 8.2.66 8.3.15	ङ् अस् इँ	भ्याम्	भ्यस्
6	कस्य 7.1.12	कयोः 7.3.104 6.1.78 8.2.66 8.3.15	केषाम् 7.1.52 7.3.103 8.3.59	(ङ्) अस्	ओस्	आम् → स् उँ ट् + आम्
7	कस्मिन् 7.1.15	कयोः 7.3.104 6.1.78 8.2.66 8.3.15	केषु 7.3.103 8.3.59	(ङ्) इ →स्मिन्	ओस्	सु
Interrogative pronouns do not have Vocative. Declines as क – अकारान्त, सर्व (called मकारान्त due to ganapatha entry किम्)						

Numeral Cardinals सङ्ख्या 1, 2, 3

Cardinals means the numbers 1, 2, 3 written in words like one, two, three, etc. There is No Vocative case for Cardinals.

Following numeral stems are used in meaning other than number also.

- एक a, the, once, prior, one
- द्वि both, pair, twin, two
- प्रथम best, highest, first, 1st
- द्वितीय latter, second, 2nd
- चतुर्थ transcendental state, fourth, 4th
- अष्टन् maya, eighth, 8th

Rest of the stems are strictly numerals in classical usage, but in Vedic usage other meanings may also be associated.

एक one

एक	अकारान्तः	अ	mfn
singular	m 1	f 1	n 1
1	एकः	एका	एकम्
2	एकम्	एकाम्	एकम्
3	एकेन	एकया	एकेन
4	एकस्मै	एकस्यै	एकस्मै
5	एकस्मात्	एकस्याः	एकस्मात्
6	एकस्य	एकस्याः	एकस्य
7	एकस्मिन्	एकस्याम्	एकस्मिन्
one			
नित्यमेकवचनान्तः singular case only, when used to mean numeral 1. Declines identical to सर्व in singular. No Vocative.			

द्वि two

द्वि	इकारान्तः	इ	mfn
dual	m 2	f 2	n 2
1	द्वौ	द्वे	द्वे
2	द्वौ	द्वे	द्वे
3	द्वाभ्याम्	द्वाभ्याम्	द्वाभ्याम्
4	द्वाभ्याम्	द्वाभ्याम्	द्वाभ्याम्
5	द्वाभ्याम्	द्वाभ्याम्	द्वाभ्याम्
6	द्वयोः	द्वयोः	द्वयोः
7	द्वयोः	द्वयोः	द्वयोः
two			
नित्यं द्विवचनान्तः only dual case. Never used in singular or plural.			
Declines identical to सर्व in dual just as अकारान्त mn, आकारान्त f			
It is called इकारान्त only because of Ganapatha listing.			

त्रि three

त्रि	इकारान्तः	इ	mfn
plural	m	f	n
1	त्रयः	तिस्रः	त्रीणि
2	त्रीन्	तिस्रः	त्रीणि
3	त्रिभिः	तिसृभिः	त्रिभिः
4	त्रिभ्यः	तिसृभ्यः	त्रिभ्यः
5	त्रिभ्यः	तिसृभ्यः	त्रिभ्यः
6	त्रयाणाम्	तिसृणाम्	त्रयाणाम्
7	त्रिषु	तिसृषु	त्रिषु
three			
नित्यं बहुवचनान्तः only plural case. Not in singular or dual.			
Declines like हरि for masculine, वारि for neuter, in plural.			

चतुर् four

चतुर्	रेफान्तः	र्	mfn
plural	m	f	n
1	चत्वारः	चतस्रः	चत्वारि
2	चतुरः	चतस्रः	चत्वारि
3	चतुर्भिः	चतसृभिः	चतुर्भिः
4	चतुर्भ्यः	चतसृभ्यः	चतुर्भ्यः
5	चतुर्भ्यः	चतसृभ्यः	चतुर्भ्यः
6	चतुर्णाम्	चतसृणाम्	चतुर्णाम्
7	चतुर्षु	चतसृषु	चतुर्षु
four			
नित्यं बहुवचनान्तः only plural case.			
Declines like वार् 3rd case onwards in masculine/neuter.			

पञ्चन् षन् सप्तन् – five six seven

plural	नकारान्तः न्		
mfn	पञ्चन्	षन्	सप्तन्
1	पञ्च	षट्	सप्त
2	पञ्च	षट्	सप्त
3	पञ्चभिः	षड्भिः	सप्तभिः
4	पञ्चभ्यः	षड्भ्यः	सप्तभ्यः
5	पञ्चभ्यः	षड्भ्यः	सप्तभ्यः
6	पञ्चानाम्	षण्णाम्	सप्तानाम्
7	पञ्चसु	षट्सु	सप्तसु
	five	six	seven
नित्यं बहुवचनान्तः only plural case. Identical spelling in masculine /feminine /neuter.			

अष्टन् eight

अष्टन्	नकारान्तः न् mfn	
1	अष्ट	अष्टौ
2	अष्ट	अष्टौ
3	अष्टभिः	अष्टाभिः
4	अष्टभ्यः	अष्टाभ्यः
5	अष्टभ्यः	अष्टाभ्यः
6	अष्टानाम्	अष्टानाम्
7	अष्टसु	अष्टासु
	eight	
नित्यं बहुवचनान्तः only plural case. Identical spelling in masculine /feminine /neuter. It is seen in literature with two spellings, ह्रस्वान्त ending in short vowel and दीर्घान्त long vowel.		

नवन् दशन् एकादशन् द्वादशन् – nine ten eleven twelve

plural	नकारान्तः न्			
mfn	नवन्	दशन्	एकादशन्	द्वादशन्
1	नव	दश	एकादश	द्वादश
2	नव	दश	एकादश	द्वादश
3	नवभिः	दशभिः	एकादशभिः	द्वादशभिः
4	नवभ्यः	दशभ्यः	एकादशभ्यः	द्वादशभ्यः
5	नवभ्यः	दशभ्यः	एकादशभ्यः	द्वादशभ्यः
6	नवानाम्	दशानाम्	एकादशानाम्	द्वादशानाम्
7	नवसु	दशसु	एकादशसु	द्वादशसु
	nine	ten	eleven	twelve
नित्यं बहुवचनान्तः only plural case. Identical spelling in masculine /feminine /neuter.				

त्रयोदशन् चतुर्दशन् पञ्चदशन् षोडशन् – thirteen fourteen fifteen sixteen

plural	नकारान्तः न्			
mfn	त्रयोदशन्	चतुर्दशन्	पञ्चदशन्	षोडशन्
1	त्रयोदश	चतुर्दश	पञ्चदश	षोडश
2	त्रयोदश	चतुर्दश	पञ्चदश	षोडश
3	त्रयोदशभिः	चतुर्दशभिः	पञ्चदशभिः	षोडशभिः
4	त्रयोदशभ्यः	चतुर्दशभ्यः	पञ्चदशभ्यः	षोडशभ्यः
5	त्रयोदशभ्यः	चतुर्दशभ्यः	पञ्चदशभ्यः	षोडशभ्यः
6	त्रयोदशानाम्	चतुर्दशानाम्	पञ्चदशानाम्	षोडशानाम्
7	त्रयोदशसु	चतुर्दशसु	पञ्चदशसु	षोडशसु
	thirteen	fourteen	fifteen	sixteen
नित्यं बहुवचनान्तः only plural case. Identical spelling in masculine /feminine /neuter.				

सप्तदशन् अष्टदशन् नवदशन् – seventeen eighteen nineteen

mfn	सप्तदशन्	अष्टदशन्	नवदशन्
1	सप्तदश	अष्टदश	नवदश
2	सप्तदश	अष्टदश	नवदश
3	सप्तदशभिः	अष्टदशभिः	नवदशभिः
4	सप्तदशभ्यः	अष्टदशभ्यः	नवदशभ्यः
5	सप्तदशभ्यः	अष्टदशभ्यः	नवदशभ्यः
6	सप्तदशानाम्	अष्टदशानाम्	नवदशानाम्
7	सप्तदशसु	अष्टदशसु	नवदशसु
	seventeen	eighteen	nineteen
नित्यं बहुवचनान्तः only plural case. Identical spelling in masculine /feminine /neuter.			

कति mfn – How many Number? How much Quantity?

कति	इकारान्तः इ mfn plural
1	कति
2	कति
3	कतिभिः
4	कतिभ्यः
5	कतिभ्यः
6	कतीनाम्
7	कतिषु
How many number? How much Quantity?	
नित्यं बहुवचनान्तः only plural case. Identical spelling in masculine /feminine /neuter.	

Numeral Ordinals सङ्ख्येय 1st, 2nd, 3rd

प्रथम m - First, 1st, Initial

प्रथम	प् र् अ थ् अ म् अ = masculine stem अ ending, अकारान्तः		
V हे	प्रथम 6.1.69	प्रथमौ	प्रथमे / प्रथमाः
	1	2	3
1	प्रथमः 8.2.66 8.3.15	प्रथमौ 6.1.88	प्रथमे / प्रथमाः 1.1.33 / 6.1.102 8.2.66 8.3.15
2	प्रथमम् 6.1.107	प्रथमौ 6.1.88	प्रथमान् 6.1.102 6.1.103
3	प्रथमेन 7.1.12 6.1.87 8.4.2	प्रथमाभ्याम् 7.3.102	प्रथमैः 7.1.9 6.1.88 8.2.66 8.3.15
4	प्रथमाय 7.1.13 7.3.102	प्रथमाभ्याम् 7.3.102	प्रथमेभ्यः 7.3.103 8.2.66 8.3.15
5	प्रथमात् 7.1.12 6.1.101	प्रथमाभ्याम् 7.3.102	प्रथमेभ्यः 7.3.103 8.2.66 8.3.15
6	प्रथमस्य 7.1.12	प्रथमयोः 7.3.104 6.1.78 8.2.66 8.3.15	प्रथमानाम् 7.1.54 6.4.3
7	प्रथमे 6.1.87	प्रथमयोः 7.3.104 6.1.78 8.2.66 8.3.15	प्रथमेषु 7.3.103 8.3.59
Sutra 1.1.33 gives optional forms for Nominative Singular 1/1			

प्रथमा f - First, Initial

प्रथमा	प् र् अ थ् अ म् आ = feminine stem आ ending, आकारान्तः		
V हे	प्रथमे 7.3.106 6.1.68	प्रथमे	प्रथमाः
	1	2	3
1	प्रथमा 6.1.68	प्रथमे 7.1.18 6.1.105 6.1.87	प्रथमाः 6.1.105 6.1.101 8.2.66 8.3.15
2	प्रथमाम् 6.1.107	प्रथमे 7.1.18 6.1.105 6.1.87	प्रथमाः 6.1.102 8.2.66 8.3.15
3	प्रथमया 7.3.105 6.1.78	प्रथमाभ्याम्	प्रथमाभिः 8.2.66 8.3.15
4	प्रथमायै 7.3.113 6.1.88	प्रथमाभ्याम्	प्रथमाभ्यः 8.2.66 8.3.15
5	प्रथमायाः 7.3.113 6.1.101 8.2.66 8.3.15	प्रथमाभ्याम्	प्रथमाभ्यः 8.2.66 8.3.15
6	प्रथमायाः 7.3.113 6.1.101 8.2.66 8.3.15	प्रथमयोः 7.3.105 6.1.78 8.2.66 8.3.15	प्रथमानाम् 7.1.54 6.4.3
7	प्रथमायाम् 7.3.116 7.3.113 6.1.101	प्रथमयोः 7.3.105 6.1.78 8.2.66 8.3.15	प्रथमासु
Declines identical to रमा except for 6/3			

प्रथम n - First, Initial

प्रथम	प् र् अ थ् अ म् अ = neuter stem अ ending, अकारान्तः		
V हे	प्रथम 2.3.49 7.1.24 6.1.107 6.1.69	प्रथमे	प्रथमानि
1	प्रथमम् 7.1.24	प्रथमे 7.1.19 6.1.87	प्रथमानि 7.1.20 7.1.72 6.4.8
2	प्रथमम् 7.1.24	प्रथमे 7.1.19 6.1.87	प्रथमानि 7.1.20 7.1.72 6.4.8
3	प्रथमेन 7.1.12 6.1.87	प्रथमाभ्याम् 7.3.102	प्रथमैः 7.1.9 8.2.66 6.1.88 8.3.15
4	प्रथमाय 7.1.13 7.3.102	प्रथमाभ्याम् 7.3.102	प्रथमेभ्यः 7.3.103 8.2.66 8.3.15
5	प्रथमात् 7.1.12 6.1.101	प्रथमाभ्याम् 7.3.102	प्रथमेभ्यः 7.3.103 8.2.66 8.3.15
6	प्रथमस्य 7.1.12	प्रथमयोः 7.3.104 6.1.78 8.2.66 8.3.15	प्रथमानाम् 7.1.54 6.4.3
7	प्रथमे 6.1.87	प्रथमयोः 7.3.104 6.1.78 8.2.66 8.3.15	प्रथमेषु 7.3.103 8.3.59
Declines identical to फल			

द्वितीय m – Second, 2nd, Latter तृतीय Third

द्वितीय	द् व् इ त् ई य् अ = masculine stem अ ending, अकारान्तः		
V हे	द्वितीय 6.1.69	द्वितीयौ	द्वितीयाः
	1	2	3
1	द्वितीयः 8.2.66 8.3.15	द्वितीयौ 6.1.88	द्वितीयाः 6.1.102 8.2.66 8.3.15
2	द्वितीयम् 6.1.107	द्वितीयौ 6.1.88	द्वितीयान् 6.1.102 6.1.103
3	द्वितीयेन 7.1.12 6.1.87 8.4.2	द्वितीयाभ्याम् 7.3.102	द्वितीयैः 7.1.9 6.1.88 8.2.66 8.3.15
4	द्वितीयस्मै / द्वितीयाय 1.1.33 / 7.1.13 7.3.102	द्वितीयाभ्याम् 7.3.102	द्वितीयेभ्यः 7.3.103 8.2.66 8.3.15
5	द्वितीयस्मात् / द्वितीयात् 1.1.33 / 7.1.12 6.1.101	द्वितीयाभ्याम् 7.3.102	द्वितीयेभ्यः 7.3.103 8.2.66 8.3.15
6	द्वितीयस्य 7.1.12	द्वितीययोः 7.3.104 6.1.78 8.2.66 8.3.15	द्वितीयानाम् 7.1.54 6.4.3 8.4.2
7	द्वितीयस्मिन् / द्वितीये 1.1.33 / 6.1.87	द्वितीययोः 7.3.104 6.1.78 8.2.66 8.3.15	द्वितीयेषु 7.3.103 8.3.59
Sutra 1.1.33 gives optional forms for Nominative Singular 1/1 for the stems प्रथम चरम तय(stems ending in तयप् affix) अल्प अर्ध कतिपय नेम । A Vartika तीयस्य ङित्सु वा extends it for ङित् affixes, i.e affixes having ङ् Tag letter. The Vartika applies to ordinal stems द्वितीय तृतीय ।			
Above table is for द्वितीय, and तृतीय declines identically.			

द्वितीया f – Second, 2nd, Latter तृतीया Third, 3rd

द्वितीया	द् व् इ त् ई य् आ = आकारान्तः		f
V हे	द्वितीये 7.3.106 6.1.68	द्वितीये	द्वितीयाः
1	द्वितीया 6.1.68	द्वितीये 7.1.18 6.1.105 6.1.87	द्वितीयाः 6.1.105 6.1.101 8.2.66 8.3.15
2	द्वितीयाम् 6.1.107	द्वितीये 7.1.18 6.1.105 6.1.87	द्वितीयाः 6.1.102 8.2.66 8.3.15
3	द्वितीयया 7.3.105 6.1.78	द्वितीयाभ्याम्	द्वितीयाभिः 8.2.66 8.3.15
4	द्वितीयस्यै / द्वितीयायै 1.1.33 / 7.3.113 6.1.88	द्वितीयाभ्याम्	द्वितीयाभ्यः 8.2.66 8.3.15
5	द्वितीयस्याः / द्वितीयायाः 1.1.33 / 7.3.113 6.1.101 8.2.66 8.3.15	द्वितीयाभ्याम्	द्वितीयाभ्यः 8.2.66 8.3.15
6	द्वितीयस्याः / द्वितीयायाः 1.1.33 / 7.3.113 6.1.101 8.2.66 8.3.15	द्वितीययोः 7.3.105 6.1.78 8.2.66 8.3.15	द्वितीयानाम् 7.1.54 6.4.3
7	द्वितीयस्याम् / द्वितीयायाम् 1.1.33 / 7.3.116 7.3.113 6.1.101	द्वितीययोः 7.3.105 6.1.78 8.2.66 8.3.15	द्वितीयासु
Declines identical to रमा except for 6/3. Similarly तृतीया			
Vartika तीयस्य ङित्सु वा extends extends Sutra 1.1.33 for ङित् affixes, i.e affixes having ङ् Tag letter. The Vartika applies to ordinal stems द्वितीया तृतीया ।			

द्वितीय n – Second, 2nd, Latter तृतीय Third, 3rd

द्वितीय	द् व् इ त् ई य् अ = neuter stem अ ending, अकारान्तः		
V हे	द्वितीय 6.1.69	द्वितीये	द्वितीयानि
	1	2	3
1	द्वितीयम् 8.2.66 8.3.15	द्वितीये 6.1.88	द्वितीयानि 6.1.102 8.2.66 8.3.15
2	द्वितीयम् 6.1.107	द्वितीये 6.1.88	द्वितीयानि 6.1.102 6.1.103
3	द्वितीयेन 7.1.12 6.1.87 8.4.2	द्वितीयाभ्याम् 7.3.102	द्वितीयैः 7.1.9 6.1.88 8.2.66 8.3.15
4	द्वितीयस्मै / द्वितीयाय 1.1.33 / 7.1.13 7.3.102	द्वितीयाभ्याम् 7.3.102	द्वितीयेभ्यः 7.3.103 8.2.66 8.3.15
5	द्वितीयस्मात् / द्वितीयात् 1.1.33 / 7.1.12 6.1.101	द्वितीयाभ्याम् 7.3.102	द्वितीयेभ्यः 7.3.103 8.2.66 8.3.15
6	द्वितीयस्य 7.1.12	द्वितीययोः 7.3.104 6.1.78 8.2.66 8.3.15	द्वितीयानाम् 7.1.54 6.4.3 8.4.2
7	द्वितीयस्मिन् / द्वितीये 1.1.33 / 6.1.87	द्वितीययोः 7.3.104 6.1.78 8.2.66 8.3.15	द्वितीयेषु 7.3.103 8.3.59
Declines identical to फल । Similarly तृतीया			

चतुर्थ m - Fourth, 4th, Transcendental State

चतुर्थ	च् अ त् उ र् थ् अ = masculine stem अ ending, अकारान्तः		
V हे	चतुर्थ	चतुर्थौ	चतुर्थाः
1	चतुर्थः	चतुर्थौ	चतुर्थाः
2	चतुर्थम्	चतुर्थौ	चतुर्थान्
3	चतुर्थेन	चतुर्थाभ्याम्	चतुर्थैः
4	चतुर्थाय	चतुर्थाभ्याम्	चतुर्थेभ्यः
5	चतुर्थात्	चतुर्थाभ्याम्	चतुर्थेभ्यः
6	चतुर्थस्य	चतुर्थयोः	चतुर्थानाम्
7	चतुर्थे	चतुर्थयोः	चतुर्थेषु
Declines identical to राम except 3/1, 6/3 - 8.4.2 doesn’t apply.			

तुरीय m - Fourth, 4th, Transcendental State

तुरीय	त् उ र् ई य् अ = masculine stem अ ending, अकारान्तः		
V हे	तुरीय	तुरीयौ	तुरीयाः
1	तुरीय	तुरीयौ	तुरीयाः
2	तुरीयम्	तुरीयौ	तुरीयान्
3	तुरीयेण	तुरीयाभ्याम्	तुरीयैः
4	तुरीयाय	तुरीयाभ्याम्	तुरीयेभ्यः
5	तुरीयात्	तुरीयाभ्याम्	तुरीयेभ्यः
6	तुरीयस्य	तुरीययोः	तुरीयाणाम्
7	तुरीये	तुरीययोः	तुरीयेषु
Declines identical to राम			
Synonym stem तुर्य			

चतुर्थी f – Fourth, 4th, Transcendental State

चतुर्थी	च् अ त् उ र् थ् ई = ईकारान्तः		f
V हे	चतुर्थि	चतुर्थ्यौ	चतुर्थ्यः
1	चतुर्थी	चतुर्थ्यौ	चतुर्थ्यः
2	चतुर्थीम्	चतुर्थ्यौ	चतुर्थीः
3	चतुर्थ्या	चतुर्थीभ्याम्	चतुर्थीभिः
4	चतुर्थ्यै	चतुर्थीभ्याम्	चतुर्थीभ्यः
5	चतुर्थ्याः	चतुर्थीभ्याम्	चतुर्थीभ्यः
6	चतुर्थ्याः	चतुर्थ्योः	चतुर्थीनाम्
7	चतुर्थ्याम्	चतुर्थ्योः	चतुर्थीषु
Declines identical to नदी ।			
4/1 = नदी ए 7.3.112 नदी आ ए 6.1.90 नदी ऐ 6.1.77 नद्य् ऐ = नद्यै ।			

तुरीया f – Fourth, 4th, Transcendental State

तुरीया	त् उ र् ई य् आ = आकारान्तः		f
V हे	तुरीये	तुरीये	तुरीयाः
1	तुरीया	तुरीये	तुरीयाः
2	तुरीयाम्	तुरीये	तुरीयाः
3	तुरीयया	तुरीयाभ्याम्	तुरीयाभिः
4	तुरीयायै	तुरीयाभ्याम्	तुरीयाभ्यः
5	तुरीयायाः	तुरीयाभ्याम्	तुरीयाभ्यः
6	तुरीयायाः	तुरीययोः	तुरीयाणाम्
7	तुरीयायाम्	तुरीययोः	तुरीयासु
Declines identical to रमा ।			

चतुर्थ n – Fourth, 4th, Transcendental State

चतुर्थ	च् अ त् उ र् थ् अ	अकारान्तः	n
V हे	चतुर्थ	चतुर्थे	चतुर्थानि
1	चतुर्थम्	चतुर्थे	चतुर्थानि
2	चतुर्थम्	चतुर्थे	चतुर्थानि
3	चतुर्थेन	चतुर्थाभ्याम्	चतुर्थैः
4	चतुर्थाय	चतुर्थाभ्याम्	चतुर्थेभ्यः
5	चतुर्थात्	चतुर्थाभ्याम्	चतुर्थेभ्यः
6	चतुर्थस्य	चतुर्थयोः	चतुर्थानाम्
7	चतुर्थे	चतुर्थयोः	चतुर्थेषु
Declines identical to फल			

तुरीय n – Fourth, 4th, Transcendental State

तुरीय	त् उ र् ई य् अ = neuter stem अ ending, अकारान्तः		
V हे	तुरीय	तुरीये	तुरीयाणि
1	तुरीयम्	तुरीये	तुरीयाणि
2	तुरीयम्	तुरीये	तुरीयाणि
3	तुरीयेण	तुरीयाभ्याम्	तुरीयैः
4	तुरीयाय	तुरीयाभ्याम्	तुरीयेभ्यः
5	तुरीयात्	तुरीयाभ्याम्	तुरीयेभ्यः
6	तुरीयस्य	तुरीययोः	तुरीयाणाम्
7	तुरीये	तुरीययोः	तुरीयेषु
Declines identical to फल, except 8.4.2 applies to V/3 1/3 2/3 3/1 6/3 for change of नकार to णकार ।			
Synonym stem तुर्य declines identically			

पञ्चम m - Fifth, 5th, onwards 6th, 7th... 100th etc

पञ्चम	प् अ ञ् च् अ म् अ = masculine stem अ ending, अकारान्तः		
V हे	पञ्चम	पञ्चमौ	पञ्चमाः
1	पञ्चमः	पञ्चमौ	पञ्चमाः
2	पञ्चमम्	पञ्चमौ	पञ्चमान्
3	पञ्चमेन	पञ्चमाभ्याम्	पञ्चमैः
4	पञ्चमाय	पञ्चमाभ्याम्	पञ्चमेभ्यः
5	पञ्चमात.	पञ्चमाभ्याम्	पञ्चमेभ्यः
6	पञ्चमस्य	पञ्चमयोः	पञ्चमानाम्
7	पञ्चमे	पञ्चमयोः	पञ्चमेषु
Declines identical to राम except for 3/1, 6/3 where 8.4.2 doesn't apply. Similarly all the succeeding ordinals षष्ठः सप्तमः अष्टमः नवमः दशमः ... शततमः 6th 7th 8th 9th 10th ... 100th etc.			
Ordinals 100 and above are cardinals suffixed with तम affix			

पञ्चमी f - Fifth, 5th, onwards 6th, 7th... 100th etc

पञ्चमी	प् अ ञ् च् अ म् ई = ईकारान्तः		f
V हे	पञ्चमि	पञ्चम्यौ	पञ्चम्यः
1	पञ्चमी	पञ्चम्यौ	पञ्चम्यः
2	पञ्चमीम्	पञ्चम्यौ	पञ्चमीः
3	पञ्चम्या	पञ्चमीभ्याम्	पञ्चमीभिः
4	पञ्चम्यै	पञ्चमीभ्याम्	पञ्चमीभ्यः
5	पञ्चम्याः	पञ्चमीभ्याम्	पञ्चमीभ्यः
6	पञ्चम्याः	पञ्चम्योः	पञ्चमीनाम्
7	पञ्चम्याम्	पञ्चम्योः	पञ्चमीषु
Declines identical to नदी ।			
4/1 = नदी ए 7.3.112 नदी आ ए 6.1.90 नदी ऐ 6.1.77 नद्य् ऐ = नद्यै ।			
Similarly all the succeeding ordinals षष्ठी सप्तमी अष्टमी नवमी दशमी ... शततमी 6th 7th 8th 9th 10th ... 100th etc.			
Ordinals 100 and above are cardinals suffixed with तम affix			

पञ्चम n – Fifth, 5th, onwards 6th, 7th... 100th etc

पञ्चम	प् अ ञ् च् अ म् अ = neuter stem अ ending, अकारान्तः		
V हे	पञ्चम	पञ्चमे	पञ्चमानि
1	पञ्चमम्	पञ्चमे	पञ्चमानि
2	पञ्चमम्	पञ्चमे	पञ्चमानि
3	पञ्चमेन	पञ्चमाभ्याम्	पञ्चमैः
4	पञ्चमाय	पञ्चमाभ्याम्	पञ्चमेभ्यः
5	पञ्चमात्	पञ्चमाभ्याम्	पञ्चमेभ्यः
6	पञ्चमस्य	पञ्चमयोः	पञ्चमानाम्
7	पञ्चमे	पञ्चमयोः	पञ्चमेषु
Declines identical to फल			
Similarly all the succeeding ordinals षष्ठम् सप्तमम् अष्टमम् नवमम् दशमम् ... शततमम् 6th 7th 8th 9th 10th ... 100th etc.			
Ordinals 100 and above are cardinals suffixed with तम affix			

Irregular Stems in Masc with final vowel विशेष शब्द पुंलिङ्गः

ऐक्ष्वाक m - First, 1st, Initial

ऐक्ष्वाक	ऐ क् ष् व् आ क् अ = masculine stem अ ending, अकारान्तः		
V हे	ऐक्ष्वाक	ऐक्ष्वाकौ	इक्ष्वाकवः
1	ऐक्ष्वाकः	ऐक्ष्वाकौ	इक्ष्वाकवः
2	ऐक्ष्वाकम्	ऐक्ष्वाकौ	इक्ष्वाकून्
3	ऐक्ष्वाकेण	ऐक्ष्वाकाभ्याम्	ऐक्ष्वाकुभिः
4	ऐक्ष्वाकाय	ऐक्ष्वाकाभ्याम्	ऐक्ष्वाकुभ्यः
5	ऐक्ष्वाकात्	ऐक्ष्वाकाभ्याम्	ऐक्ष्वाकुभ्यः
6	ऐक्ष्वाकस्य	ऐक्ष्वाकयोः	ऐक्ष्वाकूणाम्
7	ऐक्ष्वाके	ऐक्ष्वाकयोः	ऐक्ष्वाकुषु
Declines identical to राम singular, dual			Like गुरु plural

निर्जर m - Lord, Unageing, Never becoming old

निर्जर	न् इ र् ज् अ = masculine stem अ ending, अकारान्तः		
V हे	निर्जर	निर्जरौ / निर्जरसौ	निर्जराः / निर्जरसः
1	निर्जरः	निर्जरौ / निर्जरसौ	निर्जराः / निर्जरसः
2	निर्जरम् / निर्जरसम्	निर्जरौ / निर्जरसौ	निर्जरान् / निर्जरसः
3	निर्जरेण / निर्जरसा	निर्जराभ्याम्	निर्जरैः
4	निर्जराय / निर्जरसे	निर्जराभ्याम्	निर्जरेभ्यः
5	निर्जरात् / निर्जरसः	निर्जराभ्याम्	निर्जरेभ्यः
6	निर्जरस्य / निर्जरसः	निर्जरयोः	निर्जराणाम् / निर्जरसाम्
7	निर्जरे / निर्जरसि	निर्जरयोः	निर्जरेषु
Declines identical to राम, Optionally like वेधस् for अजादि affixes			
7.2.101 जराया जरसन्यतरस्याम् । Optionally निर्जर becomes निर्जरस् for vowel beginning affixes. Similar stems अजर विजर			

पाद m – Foot (body part), quarter

पाद	अकारान्तः	अ	m
V हे	पाद	पादौ	पादाः
1	पादः	पादौ	पादाः
2	पदम्	पादौ	पदः 2/3 (शस् affix)
3	पदा	पद्भ्याम्	पद्भिः
4	पदे	पद्भ्याम्	पद्भ्यः
5	पदः	पद्भ्याम्	पद्भ्यः
6	पदः	पदोः	पदाम्
7	पदि	पदोः	पत्सु
Declines identical to राम 1/1 to 2/2, then as सुहृद् 2/3 onwards. पाद (अकारान्त) is replaced with पद् (दकारान्त) for affixes शस् 2/3 onwards. Refer 6.1.63 पद्दन्नोमास्हृन्निशसन्यूषन्दोषन्यकञ्छकन्नुदन्नासञ्छस्प्रभृतिषु ।			

दन्त m – Tooth (body part)

दन्त	अकारान्तः	अ	m
V हे	दन्त	दन्तौ	दन्ताः
1	दन्तः	दन्तौ	दन्ताः
2	दन्तम्	दन्तौ	दतः 2/3 (शस् affix)
3	दता	दद्भ्याम् 8.2.39	दद्भिः 8.2.39
4	दते	दद्भ्याम् 8.2.39	दद्भ्यः 8.2.39
5	दतः	दद्भ्याम् 8.2.39	दद्भ्यः 8.2.39
6	दतः	दतोः	दताम्
7	दति	दतोः	दत्सु 8.2.39 8.4.55
Declines identical to राम 1/1 to 2/2, then as मरुत् 2/3 onwards.			
दन्त (अकारान्त) is replaced with दत् (तकारान्त) for affixes शस् 2/3 onwards. Refer 6.1.63			

मास m – month, 30 day period

मास	अ	अकारान्तः	m
V हे	मास	मासौ	मासाः
1	मासः	मासौ	मासाः
2	मासम्	मासौ	मासः 2/3 (शस् affix)
3	मासा	माभ्याम् 8.2.66 8.3.17 8.3.22	माभिः
4	मासे	माभ्याम् 8.2.66 8.3.17 8.3.22	माभ्यः
5	मासः	माभ्याम् 8.2.66 8.3.17 8.3.22	माभ्यः
6	मासः	मासोः 8.2.66 8.3.17 8.3.22	मासाम्
7	मासि	मासोः 8.2.66 8.3.17 8.3.22	माःसु / मास्सु 8.2.66 8.3.15 / 8.3.36
Declines identical to राम 1/1 to 2/2, then as भास् 2/3 onwards.			
मास (अकारान्त) is replaced with मास् (सकारान्त) for affixes शस् 2/3 onwards. Refer 6.1.63			

विश्वपा m - Lord, Protector of World

विश्वपा	आकारान्तः	आ	m
V हे	विश्वपाः 6.1.105	विश्वपौ	विश्वपाः
1	विश्वपाः	विश्वपौ 6.1.105 6.1.88	विश्वपाः 6.1.105 6.1.101
2	विश्वपाम् 6.1.107	विश्वपौ 6.1.105 6.1.88	विश्वपः 6.4.140
3	विश्वपा 6.4.140	विश्वपाभ्याम्	विश्वपाभिः
4	विश्वपे 6.4.140	विश्वपाभ्याम्	विश्वपाभ्यः
5	विश्वपः 6.4.140	विश्वपाभ्याम्	विश्वपाभ्यः
6	विश्वपः 6.4.140	विश्वपोः 6.4.140	विश्वपाम् 6.4.140
7	विश्वपि 6.4.140	विश्वपोः 6.4.140	विश्वपासु
सोमपा distiller शङ्खध्मा conch blower गोपा shepherd			

हाहा m – name of a celestial being, a gandharva, acclaimed musician

औडुलोमी m – born of a raft

सेनानी m - general

प्रधी m - thinker

प्रधी m - genius

वातप्रमी m - antelope

क्रोष्टु m – jackal, hyena

वर्षाभू m – frog, amphibian

स्वभू m – unborn, self born

हूहू m - name of a celestial being, a gandharva, acclaimed musician

Irregular Stems-m-final consonant

प्राञ्च् m – Eastern direction, South East Asia

प्रत्यञ्च् m - Western direction, Middle East

उदञ्च् m - Northern direction, Himalayan range

अन्वञ्च् m - Following

तिर्यञ्च् m – slithering, crawling

विभ्राज् m – Bright, luminous

युज् m - Sage

युञ्ज् m – United, together with, yoked

विश्वराज् m - emperor

सुपाद् m – one who has divine feet

पूषन् m – Sun, sustains life on earth

वृत्रहन् m – destroyer of demon Vrita, Lord Indra

दीर्घाहन् m – summer season

अर्वन् m - horse

अनर्वन् m – one who has no horse

ऋभुक्षिन् m – Lord Indra

उशनस् m – Shukracharya, preceptor of the demons

अनेहस् m - time

विश्ववाह् m – one who maintains the world, Lord Vishnu

तुरासाह् m - Lord Indra

दुह् m - milkman

द्रुह् m - enemy

अनडुह् m - ox

Irregular Stems f – final vowel

जरा f – Old, aged

Irregular Stems f – final consonant

द्वार् f – door, exit

अर्चिस् f - matchstick, flame

सजुष् f – companion, consort

उष्णिह् f – tune, metre of a verse

Irregular Stems n - विशेष शब्द नपुंसकलिङ्गः

अजर n – that doesn't age

Irregular Stems n – final consonant

प्राञ्च् प्राङ् प्रत्यङ् अन्वङ् उदङ् तिर्यङ् दुह् द्रुह् स्वनडुह्

Gender of Words Masculine/Feminine/Neuter

Sanskrit words are used in all the three genders, masculine, feminine, and neuter. Words used as Substantatives (Principal Nouns) are generally restricted to a single gender. Words used as Adjectives (Qualifying Nouns) are however used in all the three genders.

In Sanskrit, synonym gender stems.

Masculine Stem = पुंलिङ्ग प्रातिपदिक ~ पुंस् प्रातिपदिक

1st case = the masculine = पुंलिङ्गः ~ the man = पुमान्

7th case = In masculine = पुंलिङ्गे ~ पुंसि

Feminine Stem = स्त्रीलिङ्ग प्रातिपदिक ~ स्त्री प्रातिपदिक

1st case = the feminine = स्त्रीलिङ्गः ~ the woman = स्त्री

7th case = In feminine = स्त्रीलिङ्गे ~ स्त्रीयाम्

Neuter Stem = नपुंसकलिङ्ग ~ क्लीब प्रातिपदिक

1st case = the neuter = नपुंसकलिङ्गः ~ the thing क्लीबः

7th case = In neuter = नपुंसकलिङ्गे ~ क्लीबे

Masculine/Feminine/Neuter सुप् प्रत्यय table

meaning	विभक्ति	Case	सुप् Affixes with इत् Tag		
			singular	dual	plural
Agent	प्रथमा	1	सुँ	औ	जस्
Object	द्वितीया	2	अम्	औट्	शस्
Instrument	तृतीया	3	टा	भ्याम्	भिस्
Recipient	चतुर्थी	4	ङे	भ्याम्	भ्यस्
Point-of-Origin	पञ्चमी	5	ङसिँ	भ्याम्	भ्यस्
of (genitive)	षष्ठी	6	ङस्	ओस्	आम्
Locative	सप्तमी	7	ङि	ओस्	सुप्

7x3 Masculine/Feminine सुप् प्रत्यय table without Tag

meaning	विभक्ति	Case	सुप् Affixes without इत् Tag letters		
Agent	प्रथमा	1	स्	औ	अस्
Object	द्वितीया	2	अम्	औ	अस्
Instrument	तृतीया	3	आ	भ्याम्	भिस्
Recipient	चतुर्थी	4	ए	भ्याम्	भ्यस्
Point-of-Origin	पञ्चमी	5	अस्	भ्याम्	भ्यस्
of (genitive)	षष्ठी	6	अस्	ओस्	आम्
Locative	सप्तमी	7	इ	ओस्	सु

7x3 Neuter सुप् प्रत्यय table without Tag

meaning	विभक्ति	Case	सुप् Affixes without इत् Tag letters		
Agent	प्रथमा	1	स्	औ	इ
Object	द्वितीया	2	अम्	औ	इ
Instrument	तृतीया	3	आ	भ्याम्	भिस्
Recipient	चतुर्थी	4	ए	भ्याम्	भ्यस्
Point-of-Origin	पञ्चमी	5	अस्	भ्याम्	भ्यस्
of (genitive)	षष्ठी	6	अस्	ओस्	आम्
Locative	सप्तमी	7	इ	ओस्	सु

7x3 सुप् प्रत्यय Mechanics of Tag letters

<table>
<tr><td>1</td><td>स् उँ
1.3.2</td><td>औ</td><td>ज् अस्
1.3.7</td><td rowspan="7">1.3.2 उपदेशेऽजनुनासिक इत् । Anunasika is Tag
1.3.3 हलन्त्यम् । Final consonant is Tag
1.3.4 न विभक्तौ तुस्माः । Final तवर्ग म् स् is not Tag
1.3.7 चुटू । initial चवर्ग टवर्ग is Tag
1.3.8 लशक्वतद्धिते । initial ल् श् कवर्ग is Tag
1.3.9 तस्य लोपः । Tag letters get dropped</td></tr>
<tr><td>2</td><td>अम्
1.3.4</td><td>औ ट्
1.3.3</td><td>श् अस्
1.3.8</td></tr>
<tr><td>3</td><td>ट् आ
1.3.7</td><td>भ्याम्
1.3.4</td><td>भिस्
1.3.4</td></tr>
<tr><td>4</td><td>ङ् ए
1.3.8</td><td>भ्याम्
1.3.4</td><td>भ्यस्
1.3.4</td></tr>
<tr><td>5</td><td>ङ् अस् इँ
1.3.8, 1.3.2</td><td>भ्याम्
1.3.4</td><td>भ्यस्
1.3.4</td></tr>
<tr><td>6</td><td>ङ् अस्
1.3.4</td><td>ओस्
1.3.4</td><td>आम्
1.3.4</td></tr>
<tr><td>7</td><td>ङ् इ
1.3.8</td><td>ओस्
1.3.4</td><td>सु प्
1.3.3</td></tr>
</table>

सुप् प्रत्यय Affixes modified in use by Sutras

<table>
<tr><td>1</td><td>स् उँ →
drops
6.1.68</td><td>औ</td><td>जस् → शी
7.1.17,
जस् → शि
7.1.20</td><td rowspan="7">1.1.42 शि सर्वनामस्थानम् ।
6.1.68 हल्ङ्याब्भ्यो दीर्घात् सुतिस्यपृक्तं हल् ।
7.1.14 सर्वनाम्नः स्मै । Affix ङे 4/1 replaced by स्मै ।
7.1.15 ङसिङ्योः स्मात्स्मिनौ । Affix ङसिँ 5/1 replaced by स्मात् , Affix ङस् 6/1 replaced by स्मिन् ।
7.1.16 पूर्वादिभ्यो नवभ्यो वा । Affix ङसिँ 5/1 replaced by स्मात् Affix ङि 7/1 replaced by स्मिन् for the पूर्वादि nine stems, Optionally.
7.1.17 जसः शी । The जस् 1/3 affix is replaced by शी = श् ई ।
7.1.20 जश्शसोः शिः।
7.1.52 आमि सर्वनाम्नः सुट् ।
8.2.66 ससजुषो रुः ।
8.3.15 खरवसानयोर्विसर्जनीयः</td></tr>
<tr><td>2</td><td>अम्</td><td>औट्</td><td>शस् →शि
7.1.20</td></tr>
<tr><td>3</td><td>ट् आ</td><td>भ्याम्</td><td>भिस्</td></tr>
<tr><td>4</td><td>ङ् ए</td><td>भ्याम्</td><td>भ्यस्</td></tr>
<tr><td>5</td><td>ङ् अस् इँ</td><td>भ्याम्</td><td>भ्यस्</td></tr>
<tr><td>6</td><td>ङ् अस्</td><td>ओस्</td><td>आम् → साम्
7.1.52</td></tr>
<tr><td>7</td><td>ङ् इ</td><td>ओस्</td><td>सुप्</td></tr>
</table>

Masc feminine सर्वनामस्थानं प्रत्यय Sarvanamasthana Affixes

	सुप् प्रत्यय table with इत् Tag				without इत् Tag letters		
	1	2	3		1	2	3
1	सुँ 1/1	औ 1/2	जस् 1/3		स्	औ	अस्
2	अम् 2/1	औट् 2/2	शस्		अम्	औ	अस्
3	टा	भ्याम्	भिस्		आ	भ्याम्	भिस्
4	ङे	भ्याम्	भ्यस्		ए	भ्याम्	भ्यस्
5	ङसिँ	भ्याम्	भ्यस्		अस्	भ्याम्	भ्यस्
6	ङस्	ओस्	आम्		अस्	ओस्	आम्
7	ङि	ओस्	सुप्		इ	ओस्	सु

- The highlighted area is called सर्वनामस्थानं प्रत्यय for non-neuter i.e. masculine and feminine stems by Sutra 1.1.43 सुडनपुंसकस्य । सुट् is the array from सु of 1/1 till ट् of 2/2.
- Rest of the area is called असर्वनामस्थानं प्रत्यय । rest fifteen are non-Sarvanamasthana Affixes for any masculine / feminine stem.

Neuter नपुंसकस्य सर्वनामस्थानं प्रत्यय Sarvanamasthana Affixes

	सुप् प्रत्यय table with इत् Tag			without इत् Tag letters		
	1	2	3	1	2	3
1	सुँ	औ	जस् / शि 1/3	स्	औ	अस् / इ
2	अम्	औट्	शस् / शि 2/3	अम्	औ	अस् / इ
3	टा	भ्याम्	भिस्	आ	भ्याम्	भिस्
4	ङे	भ्याम्	भ्यस्	ए	भ्याम्	भ्यस्
5	ङसिँ	भ्याम्	भ्यस्	अस्	भ्याम्	भ्यस्
6	ङस्	ओस्	आम्	अस्	ओस्	आम्
7	ङि	ओस्	सुप्	इ	ओस्	सु

- 1.1.42 शि सर्वनामस्थानम् । two out of 21 affixes are called Sarvanamasthana Affixes for Neuter stems. शि is the affix replacement for जस् 1/3 & शस् 2/3 for neuter stems.

5+1 सर्वनामस्थानं प्रत्यय Sarvanamasthana Affixes

	सुप् प्रत्यय table with इत् Tag				without इत् Tag letters		
	1	2	3		1	2	3
1	सुँ	औ	जस् / शि		स्	औ	अस् / इ
2	अम्	औट्	शस् / शि		अम्	औ	अस् / इ
3	टा	भ्याम्	भिस्		आ	भ्याम्	भिस्
4	ङे	भ्याम्	भ्यस्		ए	भ्याम्	भ्यस्
5	ङसिँ	भ्याम्	भ्यस्		अस्	भ्याम्	भ्यस्
6	ङस्	ओस्	आम्		अस्	ओस्	आम्
7	ङि	ओस्	सुप्		इ	ओस्	सु

If any Sutra says it applies to non-SarvanamaSthana sffixes, then this table is helpful. Conversely if any Sutra says it applies to SarvanamaSthana affixes, then too this table can be used. (i.e. sutras where gender is not specified).

हलादि प्रत्यय Affixes having Initial Consonant

Case	सुप् प्रत्यय table with इत् Tag				without इत् Tag letters		
	1	2	3		1	2	3
1	सुँ	औ	जस्		स्	औ	अस्
2	अम्	औट्	शस्		अम्	औ	अस्
3	टा	भ्याम्	भिस्		आ	भ्याम्	भिस्
4	ङे	भ्याम्	भ्यस्		ए	भ्याम्	भ्यस्
5	ङसिँ	भ्याम्	भ्यस्		अस्	भ्याम्	भ्यस्
6	ङस्	ओस्	आम्		अस्	ओस्	आम्
7	ङि	ओस्	सुप्		इ	ओस्	सु

- Highlighted Affixes are the Consonant beginning हलादि असर्वनामस्थानं प्रत्यय । Any Anga that faces these during word construction is called पद । These are named after leaving out the Sarvanamsthana affixes. By Sutra 1.4.17 the Anga is called "पद" facing भ्याम् भिस् भ्याम् भ्यस् भ्याम् भ्यस् सु affixes.
- Unmarked affixes are the vowel beginning अजादि असर्वनामस्थानं प्रत्यय । Anga facing them is called भ । By Sutra 1.4.18 the Anga is called "भ" facing अस् आ ए अस् अस् ओस् आम् इ ओस् affixes.

This is done for application of correct sandhi rule. Definition of Anga is the Entity that is facing an Affix during word construction. Thus Anga is an unfinished word that can be

- Root
- Root + affix
- Root + augment + affix

that is now facing a new affix.

Anga facing these Sup affixes gets पदम् Technical Name

Case	सुप् प्रत्यय table with इत् Tag				without इत् Tag letters		
	1	2	3		1	2	3
1							
2							
3		भ्याम्	भिस्			भ्याम्	भिस्
4		भ्याम्	भ्यस्			भ्याम्	भ्यस्
5		भ्याम्	भ्यस्			भ्याम्	भ्यस्
6							
7			सुप्				सु

These are consonant-beginning non-Sarvanamasthana affixes. By 1.4.17 स्वादिष्वसर्वनामस्थाने and 1.4.18 यचि भम् । Note that finished words are also called पदम् by 1.4.14 सुप्तिङन्तं पदम् ।

mf Anga facing these Sup affixes gets भ Technical Name

Case	सुप् प्रत्यय table with इत् Tag				without इत् Tag letters		
	1	2	3		1	2	3
1							
2							
3	टा				आ		
4	ङे				ए		
5	ङसिँ				अस्		
6	ङस्	ओस्	आम्		अस्	ओस्	आम्
7	ङि	ओस्			इ	ओस्	

These are vowel-beginning non-Sarvanamasthana affixes.

By 1.4.18 यचि भम् । This is an exception to 1.4.17, hence 1.4.17 gets applied only to consonant-beginning.

See the application of Sandhi Rules:

- रामेन $^{3/1}$ by णत्वम् sandhi → रामेण ।
- Also in 7/3 form by षटुत्वम् sandhi रामेसु → रामेषु ।
- See मरुत् due to जश्त्वम् sandhi where झर् follows, there त् → द् and some places again the द् → त् due to चर्त्वम् sandhi.

A category of stems and words in Paninian Grammar are given the type of Sarvanama. These can be loosely translated to Pronouns in English, and many words in this category are actually Pronouns. However, Panini has made the सर्वनाम category to specifically provide the appropriate affixes for their correct declension.

In the Sup affixes table, there are 7x3 = 21 basic affixes. The words that fall under the Sarvanam category, by Sutra 1.1.27 सर्वादीनि सर्वनामानि । are all listed in the Ganapatha. These words have the first 5 Sup affixes modified out of the 21. E.g.

- the word राम is not of the pronoun category. It will take the 1/3 sup affix जस् ।
- the word सर्व belongs to the pronoun category. It wil take the modified 1/3 sup affix शि by sutra 1.1.42 शि सर्वनामस्थानम् ।

Karaka Vibhakti table

1	Subject, agent	Denoted by verb
2	Object	Accusative
3	By, with	Instrumental
4	To, for	Recipient
5	From, out of, than	Point-of-origin
6	Of, 's, among	Genitive (no karaka, unrelated to verb)
7	In, at, on	Locus

कारक-विभक्तिः

1	कर्त्ता	ने
2	कर्म	को
3	करणम्	से, के साथ
4	सम्प्रदानम्	के लिए, को
5	अपादानम्	से शुरु
6		
7	अधिकरणम्	मे, पर

For Understanding cases विभक्तिः , ask the correct Question. The verb क्रिया is the fulcrum कारक , that is denoted by every case except the 6th case. Let us use the Root दा to give, ददाति gives.

1	who	कः ददाति
2	what	किम् ददाति
3	how	केन ददाति
4	To whom	कस्मै ददाति
5	from	कस्मात् ददाति
6		
7	Where, when	कुत्र , कदा ददाति

- Rama gives a book by hand from his bag to a friend in the temple. In Sanskrit we write this sentence commonly as: In the temple, Rama from his bag, to a friend, by hand, a book gives.
- देवालये रामः स्युतात् मित्राय हस्तेन पुस्तकम् ददाति ।
- In the kitchen, Sita gave from the plate, with a ladle, sweets to Lata. पाकशालायां सीता स्थालिकायाः लतायै दर्व्या मधुरं ददाति ।

Karaka = the factors related to action, i.e. the nouns related to the verb.
The 6th case is not related to the verb, rather it is related to another noun in the sentence.

In any sentence, what is denoted by the verb takes 1st case.
In active voice कर्त्तरि, the agent is denoted and takes 1st case.

In passive voice कर्मणि, the object is denoted and takes 1st case, while agent takes 3rd case.

Relevant Ashtadhyayi Sutras

6.1.68	हल्ङ्याब्भ्यो दीर्घात् सुतिस्यपृक्तं हल् ।
8.2.39	झलां जशोऽन्ते । Final झल् of word is replaced with corresponding जश् letter. झल् = row consonant letters except nasals, and sibilants and aspirate. जश् = 3rd letter of row consonant = ग् ज् ड् द् ब् । Thus, Final क् ख् ग् घ् is replaced with ग् । Final च् छ् ज् झ् is replaced with ज् । Final ट् ठ् ड् ढ् is replaced with ड् । Final त् थ् द् ध् is replaced with द् । Final प् फ् ब् भ् is replaced with ब् । Final श् is replaced with ज् । Place of utterance = Palata Final ष् is replaced with ड् । Place of utterance = Cerebrum Final स् is replaced with द् । Place of utterance = Teeth Final ह् is replaced with ग् । Place of utterance = Throat
8.2.66	ससजुषो रुः ।
8.3.15	खरवसानयोर्विसर्जनीयः ।
8.4.55	खरि च ।
8.4.56	वाऽवसाने ।

Relevant Technical Terms

पदम् (final word)	1.4.14 सुप्तिङन्तं पदम् । entity ending in सुप् / तिङ्
पदम् (anga)	1.4.17 स्वादिष्वसर्वनामस्थाने । entity that which faces initial-consonant-affix
भम् (anga)	1.4.18 यचि भम् । entity that which faces initial-vowel-affix

सर्वनामस्थानम्	1.1.42 शि सर्वनामस्थानम् । affixes for neuter stems
सर्वनामस्थानम्	1.1.43 सुडनपुंसकस्य । affixes for non-neuter stems
सम्बुद्धिः	एकवचनं सम्बुद्धिः । Vocative Singular

Place & Effort of Enunciation

Place of speech	Vowels स्वर		Row Consonants व्यञ्जन Alpaprana / Mahaprana					Semi vowel	Sibilant
			A	M	A	M	A	A	M
	Short	Long	1st	2nd	3rd	4th	5th		
कण्ठ	अ	आ	क	ख	ग	घ	ङ		ह
तालु	इ	ई	च	छ	ज	झ	ञ	य	श
मूर्धा	ऋ	ॠ	ट	ठ	ड	ढ	ण	र	ष
दन्त	ऌ		त	थ	द	ध	न	ल	स
ओष्ठ	उ	ऊ	प	फ	ब	भ	म		
Consonants are supplied with vowel अ to aid enunciation									

कण्ठ – तालु	ए ऐ	Diphthongs have twin places of utterance, being compound vowels
कण्ठ – ओष्ठ	ओ औ	
दन्त – ओष्ठ	व	The vakara is different from the other semivowels as it has twin places of utterance
नासिक्य	ं , अं	Anusvara is a pure Nasal
अनुनासिका	ँ , ॐ , यँ	Candrabindu means Nasalization

<table>
<tr><td rowspan="2">कण्ठ
Soft, Mahaprana</td><td>ह्</td><td>Hakara is an Aspirate. It is sounded like a soft release of breath</td></tr>
<tr><td>◌ः</td><td>Visarga is an Aspirate. It is sounded like ह् along with its preceding vowel</td></tr>
<tr><td colspan="3">Ardha Visarga ◌ः is also written as ᳵ</td></tr>
<tr><td>Base of tongue
Hard, Alpaprana</td><td>◌ः or ᳵ</td><td>Jihvamuliya pronounce as ह्
(a visarga preceding क , ख)</td></tr>
<tr><td>ओष्ठ
Hard, Alpaprana</td><td>◌ः or ᳵ</td><td>Upadhmaniya pronounce as फ्
(a visarga preceding प , फ)</td></tr>
</table>

कण्ठ्य Guttural or Velar	तालव्य Palatal	मूर्धन्य Cerebral or Retroflex or Lingual	दन्त्य Dental	ओष्ठ्य Labial

Maheshwar Sutras w.r.t. Pratyaharas

SN	Sutra	Pratyahara (Letter Array)	Count
1	अ इ उ ण्	अण्	1
2	ऋ ऌ क्	अक् इक् उक्	3
3	ए ओ ङ्	एङ्	1
4	ऐ औ च्	अच् इच् एच् ऐच्	4
5	ह य व र ट्	अट्	1
6	लँ ण्	अण् इण् यण् (रँ)	3
7	ञ म ङ ण न म्	अम् यम् ङम् (ञम्)	3
8	झ भ ञ्	यञ्	1
9	घ ढ ध ष्	झष् भष्	2
10	ज ब ग ड द श्	अश् हश् वश् झश् जश् बश्	6
11	ख फ छ ठ थँ च ट त व्	छव् (खँ)	1
12	क प य्	यय् मय् झय् खय् (चय्) (जय्)	4
13	श ष स र्	यर् झर् खर् चर् शर्	5
14	ह ल्	अल् हल् वल् रल् झल् शल्	6
		Basic Count of Pratyahara =	41
Extended Count 41 + ③ = 44, with later grammarians +2 = 46			

Latin Transliteration Chart

International Alphabet of Sanskrit Transliteration (I.A.S.T.)

a	ā	i	ī	u	ū	ṛ	ṝ	ḷ	
अ	आ	इ	ई	उ	ऊ	ऋ	ॠ	ऌ	
						◌ृ	◌ॄ	◌ॢ	
e	ai	o	au	ṃ	m̐	ḥ	Ardha Visarga	oṃ	
ए	ऐ	ओ	औ	◌ं	◌ँ	◌ः	ᳲ	ॐ	
Consonants are shown with vowel 'a = अ' for uttering									
ka	क	ca	च	ṭa	ट	ta	त	pa	प
kha	ख	cha	छ	ṭha	ठ	tha	थ	pha	फ
ga	ग	ja	ज	ḍa	ड	da	द	ba	ब
gha	घ	jha	झ	ḍha	ढ	dha	ध	bha	भ
ṅa	ङ	ña	ञ	ṇa	ण	na	न	ma	म
ya	ra	la	va		ḷa	'			
य	र	ल	व		ळ	ऽ			
					Consonant only				
śa	ṣa	sa	ha		ka	क्अ = क			
श	ष	स	ह		k	क्			

The symbol ꣳ is pronounced as गुं guṃ. It is an ayogavaha अयोगवाह sound seen in Vedic literature due to Sandhi.

Sanskrit Grammar

Sandhis separated word by word पदच्छेद (प०),

Verses in prose order अन्वय (अ०),and with विभक्ति Cases.

Abbreviations

Nouns

m masculine, **f** feminine, **n** neuter; **V** vocative

1/1 = vibhakti case from 1 to 7/number 1 to 3

Indeclinables (uninflected nouns or verbs) **0**

In Sanskrit the **adverbs** are mostly uninflected.

Verbs

iii/1 = person i to iii / number 1 to 3

PPP = Past Participle Passive = क्त

PPA = Past Participle Active = क्तवत्

PrPA = PresentParticiple Active = शतृ/ शानच्

PoPP = PotentialParticiple Passive = य, तव्य, अनीयर् (gerund)

तुमुन् = infinitive, in the sense of "to do"

Anusvara and Makara have been kept as they are in Padacheda, to avoid over work. E.g. इदं should be written as इदम् in Padacheda.

Sanskrit Literature frequently omits the verb – "is". The words भवति, अस्ति etc. are implicit.

Since Sanskrit is an inflectional language, the **spelling of the same word** changes as per context or usage. Hence words can be **placed anywhere** in a sentence, as in poetic use, without change in meaning. The matrix shows how.

Verb inflections in Sanskrit – a sample chart

982 गमॢ गतौ – to go, also in the sense of attainment			
Present Tense Active voice लट् कर्तरि प्रयोगः			
Person/no	singular	dual	plural
Third	गच्छति[iii/1]	गच्छतः[iii/2]	गच्छन्ति[iii/3]
Second	गच्छसि[ii/1]	गच्छथः[ii/2]	गच्छथ [ii/3]
First	गच्छामि[i/1]	गच्छावः [i/2]	गच्छामः[i/3]

Noun declensions in Sanskrit – a sample chart

Masculine stem, vowel अending			
(र्–आ–म्–अ) राम[m] Lord's name			
	singular[1]	dual [2]	plural [3]
Vocative	हे राम[V/1]	हे रामौ[V/2]	हे रामाः[V/3]
1 Doer	रामः[1/1]	रामौ[1/2]	रामाः[1/3]
2 Object	रामम्[2/1]	रामौ[2/2]	रामान्[2/3]
3 by	रामेण[3/1]	रामाभ्याम्[3/2]	रामैः[3/3]
4 for	रामाय[4/1]	रामाभ्याम्[4/2]	रामेभ्यः[4/3]
5 from	रामात्[5/1]	रामाभ्याम् [5/2]	रामेभ्यः[5/3]
6 of	रामस्य[6/1]	रामयोः[6/2]	रामाणाम्[6/3]
7 in	रामे[7/1]	रामयोः[7/2]	रामेषु[7/3]

Masculine stem, consonant त् ending			
मरुत्^{m} Wind, Breeze, Air			
	singular[1]	dual [2]	plural [3]
Vocative	हे मरुत्$^{V/1}$	हे मरुतौ$^{V/2}$	हे मरुतः$^{V/3}$
1 Doer	मरुत् $^{1/1}$	मरुतौ $^{1/2}$	मरुतः $^{1/3}$
2 Object	मरुतम् $^{2/1}$	मरुतौ $^{2/2}$	मरुतः$^{2/3}$
3 by	मरुता $^{3/1}$	मरुद्भ्याम्$^{3/2}$	मरुद्भिः $^{3/3}$
4 for	मरुते $^{4/1}$	मरुद्भ्याम्$^{4/2}$	मरुद्भ्यः$^{4/3}$
5 from	मरुतः $^{5/1}$	मरुद्भ्याम्$^{5/2}$	मरुद्भ्यः$^{5/3}$
6 of	मरुतः $^{6/1}$	मरुतोः$^{6/2}$	मरुताम्$^{6/3}$
7 in	मरुति $^{7/1}$	मरुतोः$^{7/2}$	मरुत्सु $^{7/3}$

Moods and Tenses in Sanskrit

1	लट्	Present Tense
2	लुङ्	Aorist Past Tense,*before from now onwards*
3	लङ्	Imperfect Past Tense – *before from yesterday onwards*
4	लिट्	Perfect Past Tense – *distant unseen past*
5	लृट्	Simple Future Tense – *now onwards*
6	लुट्	Periphrastic Future Tense – *tomorrow onwards*
7	लृङ्	Conditional Mood - *if/then in past or future*
8	लोट्	Imperative Mood – *request*
9	विधि–लिङ्	Potential Mood – *order विधिलिङ्* (also known as Optative Mood)
10	आशीर्–लिङ्	Benedictive Mood – *blessing आशीर्लिङ्* (also used in the sense of a curse)

Conjugation process of Verb

वदन्ति = they say, they describe. 1st conjugation Root, Parasmaipadi.

1009 √ वदँ व्यक्तायां वाचि । to tell, relate, describe.

1.3.1 भूवादयो धातवः। वदँ = वद्अँ ।

1.3.2 उपदेशेऽजनुनासिक इत् । 1.3.9 तस्य लोपः। वद् ।

3.4.69 लः कर्मणि च भावे चाकर्मकेभ्यः। वद् ।

3.2.123 वर्तमाने लट् । 3.4.77 लस्य । वद् + लँट् ।

1.3.3 हलन्त्यम् । 1.3.9 तस्य लोपः । वद्+लँ ।

1.3.2 उपदेशेऽजनुनासिक इत् । 1.3.9तस्य लोपः । वद्+ल् ।

3.4.78 तिप्तस्झिसिप्थस्थमिब्वस्मस् तातांझथासाथांध्वमिड्वहिमहिङ् ।

1.4.199 लः परस्मैपदम् । choose Parasmaipada affix.

वद्+झि । we are conjugating third person

1.4.101 तिङस्त्रीणि त्रीणि प्रथममध्यमोत्तमाः ।

1.4.102 तान्येकवचनद्विवचनबहुवचनान्येकशः । वद्+झि । plural

1.4.108 शेषे प्रथमः । वद्+झि । this is called "प्रथमः" i.e. the **first and most** used in language, third person.

3.4.113 तिङ्शित्सार्वधातुकम् । वद्+झि ।

3.1.68 कर्त्तरि शप् । वद्+शप्+झि ।

3.4.113तिङ्शित्सार्वधातुकम् । वद्+शप्+झि ।

7.1.3 झोऽन्तः । वद्+शप्+ अन्ति ।

1.3.3 हलन्त्यम्। 1.3.8लशक्वतद्धिते। 1.3.9तस्य लोपः।वद्+अ+अन्ति ।

6.1.97 अतो गुणे । वद्+अन्ति । sandhi drops the अकारः ।

8.3.24 नश्चापदान्तस्य झलि । वद् + अंति । Anusvara appears

8.4.58 अनुस्वारस्य ययि परसवर्णः । वद् + अन्ति । Anusvara changes to नकारः ।

वद् + अन्ति = वदन्ति iii/3 लट् । iii = 3rd person, 3 = plural.
Third person plural, Present Tense.

Declension process of Noun

ब्रह्म = Brahma. The Lord. Highest Intelligence.

Stem Brahmanब्रह्मन् n → ब्रह्म neuter Nominative $^{1/1}$
The Great Lord. The Invisible presence.

1.2.45 अर्थवदधातुरप्रत्ययः प्रातिपदिकम् । ब्रह्मन्

1.2.46 कृत्तद्धितसमासाश्च । 3.1.1 प्रत्ययः । 3.1.2 परश्च ।

4.1.1 ङ्याप्प्रातिपदिकात् । 4.1.2 स्वौजस-

मौट्छष्टाभ्याम्भिस्ङेभ्याम्भ्यस्ङसिभ्याम्भ्यस्ङसोसाम्ङ्योस्सुप् ।

1.4.104विभक्तिश्च । 1.4.103 सुपः = use one of these vibhakti suffix. ब्रह्मन्

\+ सुँ ।

1.4.22 द्व्येकयोर्द्विवचनैकवचने = singular number taken.

ब्रह्मन् + सुँ ।

7.1.23 स्वमोर्नपुंसकात् । 2.4.13 यस्मात्प्रत्ययविधिस्तदादि प्रत्ययेऽङ्गम् । 6.4.1

अङ्गस्य । 1st and 2nd case Vibhakti drops for neuter stem. ब्रह्मन् ।

1.4.17 स्वादिष्वसर्वनामस्थाने । The word gets पदसंज्ञा ।

ब्रह्मन् ।

8.2.7 न लोपः प्रातिपदिकान्तस्य । Final नकार drops.

ब्रह्म $^{n1/1}$ ।

Neuter. First case nominative singular. **Brahma**.

The Highest. The Supreme. Shiva. Purusha. Tao.
The Beautiful, The Love, The Infinite, The Divine.
Any name is **Him**.
All directions point to **It**. Every form is **She**.

References

Author	Title	Ed.	Year	Publisher
KLV Sastry & Anantarama Sastri	Sabda Manjari Reprint - 2013	1st	1961	RS Vadhyar & Sons, Palghat.
Avanindra Kumar	अष्टाध्यायी पदानुक्रम कोश	2nd	2008	Parimal Publications, Delhi
Pushpa Dikshit	शीघ्रबोध व्याकरणम्	2nd	2017	Pratibha Prakashan, Delhi
	अष्टाध्यायी सहजबोध Vol 5	1st	2016	
Ashwini Kumar Aggarwal	Dhatupatha of Panini	2nd	2017	Devotees of Sri Sri Ravi Shankar Ashram, Punjab
	The Sanskrit Alphabet	1st	2017	
	Maheshwar Sutras Pratyaharas	1st	2018	
	Sanskrit Sandhi Handbook	1st	2019	
	Sanskrit Nouns Sabda Manjari	1st	2019	

Online Links
http://bhagavadgita.org.in/declension
https://www.learnsanskrit.cc/
http://sanskrit.uohyd.ac.in/scl/#
https://www.sanskritworld.in/index/Sanskrittool
http://sanskrit.jnu.ac.in/index.jsp
http://sanskrit.segal.net.br/
https://ashtadhyayi.com/

Epilogue

Knowing the sutras behind the Nouns is serious and time-consuming work, yet it bestows immense satisfaction.

Hope this work delights and cheers every Vyakarana enthusiast.

सर्वे भवन्तु सुखिनः । सर्वे सन्तु निरामयाः ।

सर्वे भद्राणि पश्यन्तु । मा कश्चिद् दुःख भाग्भवेत् ॥

ॐ शान्तिः शान्तिः शान्तिः ॥

When faith has blossomed in life, Every step is led by the Divine.
Sri Sri Ravi Shankar

Om Namah Shivaya

जय गुरुदेव

www.ingramcontent.com/pod-product-compliance
Lightning Source LLC
LaVergne TN
LVHW010551160826
845677LV00013B/3080